ROLLER SKATING GUIDE

ROLLER SKATING GUIDE

Hal Straus &
Marilou Sturges

ANDERSON WORLD, INC.

Mountain View, California

Library of Congress Cataloging in Publication Data

Straus, Hal, 1947-
  Roller skating guide.

  Includes index.
  1. Roller skating. I. Sturges, Marilou, 1952-
joint author. II. Title.
GV859.S77   796.2'1   78-68563
ISBN 0-89037-203-9

Second Printing, May 1980

Anderson World, Inc.
P.O. Box 159, Mountain View, CA 94042

For Jane, Fred, Lil, and Lou

Contents

Acknowledgments

Special thanks to the following people, without whom this book could not have been written: Tommy Andrew and Jim and Suzy Pollard of the Redwood Roller Rink, Redwood City, California; Joe Nazzaro, Life Member of the SRSTA and RSROA and certainly owner of the title "Mr. Roller Skating"; beautiful and patient champion Bettie Jennings; Dr. Allen Selner; and Lee Cole and Richard Nanini of Skates on Haight, San Francisco.

We wish to thank the following for their generous time, advice, and contributions: George Pickard, Executive Director of the RSROA; Susan Theis, Senior Editor of *Skate* magazine; Grady Merrell of Skate Ranch, Santa Ana; Ron Jerue of Holiday Skating Plaza, Sacramento; ace photographers David K. Madison, Bob Kingsbook, and Damon Webster; Ron Jellse, Harp's Rollerdrome, Cincinnati; Dan King of King's Skate County, Sacramento; Fred Bergin; David Lipschultz and William McCoy of the International Skating League; our graceful models Margo and Steve Lister, Tom Bittner, and Suzi Skates.

Grateful acknowledgment to the Roller Skating Rink Operators Association and *Skate* magazine for permission to reprint previously published material, and to the many manufacturers and distributors of roller skating equipment who sent us materials.

PART 1

LET'S GET THINGS ROLLING!

1

Roller Boom

As it did more than a half-century ago, America has taken to putting wheels under its collective feet. Not the rubber tire variety this time, but a substance called *polyurethane,* a smooth plastic compound now used to make outdoor roller-skate wheels —and an innovation many claim has transformed this once forgotten pastime into America's newest multimillion-dollar sports craze.

Stroll on down to Golden Gate Park in San Francisco, Central Park in New York, the Santa Monica boardwalk in Los Angeles—or any of the thousands of new or renovated indoor rinks—and you will witness the Roller Boom!: hundreds of youngsters, teensters, and oldsters gliding gracefully along their merry way. Some are hunched in speed-skating style as they zoom down hills of asphalt, others sail smoothly into camel spins and pirouettes, all of them smiling to the melody of some invisible, inner music (and in the case of the many skaters with stereo-headphones clamped over their ears, not invisible at all).

Yet roller skating has not glided into the American sports spotlight out of the blue. As the country has developed concern for health and exercise, and the desire and opportunity for leisure and recreation, roller skating can be viewed as a very natural culmination of both impulses. The sport combines the exercise, endurance-enhancing capacities, and exhilaration of running, the daredevil thrills of skateboarding, and the artistic dimensions of ice figure and dance skating.

The roller boom hits San Francisco's Golden Gate Park.

Roller skaters may not outnumber runners, but they are giving them a run for their money. Olympic team physician Dr. Max Novich has been quoted as saying:

> With medical authority, I can tell you that roller-skating encompasses the same benefits as jogging but with less effort . . . . It takes longer through roller skating to accomplish the same thing that running does, but for people who haven't used their muscles, roller skating is better.

And when the President's Council on Physical Fitness surveyed medical experts to evaluate the health qualities of fourteen sports, only jogging and bicycling came out ahead overall (*Resident and Staff Physician,* 1977).

A SOCIAL SPORT

Roller skaters come in all shapes, sizes, and ages. Statistics compiled by the Roller Skating Rink Operators Association indicate that more than twenty million people participate annually, and that almost one-third are under 12 years of age. Roller skating is a family sport; believe it or not, your grandpa and grandma skated before you were born and still might be now—as a recreation-exercise for senior citizens, roller skating is unsurpassed.

And yet roller skating can also be intensely, creatively individualistic. Watch the spins, turns, and dance movements of the more artistic skaters and you will get a glimpse of the dynamic possibilities.

Even better, rent a pair of skates at your nearest rink or skate shop (usually a reasonable $1.00 to $1.50 per hour) and try out a few whirls and twirls yourself. You might have a bit of trouble now, but after reading this book, you will be zooming, cameling and roller-discoing with the best of them.

Socialites and celebrities seem perfectly at ease in exhibiting their wares at roller rinks. Lily Tomlin, Richard Harris, Joan Hackett, and Olivia Newton-John have been photographed skating in rollarenas and in the newest fantasy faires "Roller Discos." On a recent Linda Ronstadt album cover, the singer balances precariously on skates, bracing herself on the walls of a narrow hallway, a paradoxical wing-footed star with a "fear of skating."

Ms. Suzi Skates.

Call the Roll!

• In San Francisco, Ms. Suzi Skates is the diva of a new sport she calls "street skating." She has started her own business as a skate messenger and is a one-woman skating show as she glides up and down San Francisco's dizzying hills. "It is a form of transportation," she says in *Roller Skating* magazine.

"If I want to get some place, I skate. It's both more fun and faster than walking."

• In 1976, the *National Observer* reported that roller skating is second only to bowling in popular participation.

• *Time* magazine noted in 1978 that roller skating is becoming the new mode of transportation in many rush-hour, traffic-congested cities. (Commuterrollers?)

• In many cities, park drive-throughs have been shut down on weekends for the use of roller skaters.

"Skating makes people feel happy," says Teresa Schneider of Sun Skates in Santa Cruz. "It's a healthy invigorating sport. Even people who've never skated before can learn it on their own, usually in just a couple of hours. I know one guy who tried it out, sold his car, and now skates to work each day. He figured it was the only way to go."

The roller rink of today (Skate *Magazine*).

A family out for a Sunday skate.

A YEAR-ROUND SPORT

Unlike ice skating, which is difficult and expensive to simulate indoors, roller skating is a year-round sport, indoors and out. There are now more than three thousand rinks in the United States—not the drafty gang hangouts one commonly misassociates with roller skating, but modern well-lit, smooth epoxy-sliding rollarenas. Organ music by Aunt Miriam has been replaced by rock music by Phil Spector, the three-stooled hot-dog snack bar by the soft-light bar lounge, the revolving Stardust ballroom ceiling fixture with multicolored flashing light shows that keep rhythm with the pulsating music.

In New York, Los Angeles, and other major cities, the roller disco phenomenon has turned rock 'n rollers to rockin' roller skaters. Dancing on your feet can be smooth and easy, but slidin' 'n glidin', movin' 'n groovin' at twenty miles an hour can be something else entirely.

Glidin' on wheels beats hoppin' on heels (RSROA).

Yes, the Roller Boom is rolling along at top speed. But how has it all evolved? What of the history of this exciting new sport? Aha! That's just it. It's not a "new" sport at all.

It all began in the early 1700s when . . .

2

Rolling Back Through the Corridors of Time

An anonymous Dutchman invented what was probably the first roller skate by nailing wooden spools to strips of wood and then attaching these contraptions to his shoes. No doubt an attempt to "summerize" winter ice skating, it was probably an unsatisfactory one, for there was nothing more recorded on the subject for fifty years.

In 1760, an eccentric Belgian musician-inventor, Joseph Merlin, concocted the first metal-wheeled skate. Obviously not one for modest previews, he debuted his invention at a fashionable London masquerade party while at the same time playing his violin—and promptly crashed into a $1300 mirror, inflicting unspecified damage to himself, the mirror, the violin, and the first metal-wheel roller skate.

In his excitement over his new invention he forgot to include on the skate some means for stopping or turning.

Unsurprisingly, no more was heard about roller skating until 1790 when a Parisian diemaker named Vanlende came up with another type of wheeled skate called the *patin-a-terre* or "ground skate." Once again, the invention was probably not the pinnacle of technological craftsmanship—roller skating again disappeared almost entirely from public attention for twenty-eight years. Then, in 1818, after skates were used in a ballet performance in Berlin to simulate ice skating, roller skating emerged as an integral part of novelty acts in Paris, used in exhibitions, carnivals, and other similar entertainments.

The ostentatious debut of the first roller skates.

In 1919, skaters appeared on the streets of Paris—and a Monsieur Petitbled was granted the first roller skate patent.

Opera Pushes Skating Over the Edge

The primary reason behind roller skating's cultural ups and downs was the important functional defect in these early skates—some means for stopping and turning. Patterned on the bladed ice skate, the wheels were aligned three or four in a row on the bottom of the skate, allowing no pivot for turning except by brute strength.

An English inventor, Robert John Tyers, imagined he discovered a marvelous solution: He enlarged the middle wheel so that the skater would have a fulcrum on which to turn. His "Volito" skate also had brakes—hooks that dragged in the front and back. However, what this new feature achieved in ingenuity it lost in balance—when the skater leaned forward or backward in order to turn, he was left with only two wheels to accomplish it, a bravura feat more in tune with tightrope walking than the graceful glides and arabesques of artistic roller skating.

Interestingly enough, roller skating received its biggest public push in the nineteenth century from the milieu of high-brow culture—the opera. To simulate ice skating scenes, roller skates were used in Meyerbeer's *Le Prophete* at the Paris Opera House in 1849 and in Taglioni's *Le Plaisir de l'hiver, ou Les Patineurs* (The Pleasures of Winter, or the Skaters) a few years later in London. The public reaction to these two productions was enthusiastic enough (at least in laughter—the performers often rolled off the stage into the orchestra pit) to encourage London impressarios to build the first roller skating rinks in 1857.

An artist's conception of the Tyers roller skate.

Good Ol' American Ingenuity

If anyone is the father of modern roller skating, it is James Leonard Plimpton, whose 1863 four-wheeled "rocking skate" (tagged as such by Charles Dickens in a London newspaper) finally solved the turning defect; with his new "parallel wheels" feature, skaters had only to lean to one side or the other for turning in wide arcs. Moreover, the skates had rubber "action" pads for turning; the plates and wheels were made of wood. The Plimpton skate developed into the direct predecessor of the skate used for the next hundred years.

Plimpton's invention sparked the first worldwide roller boom in the early 1870s. His $100,000 roller rink in New York City

The Plimpton skate.

and lush summer rink in Newport, Rhode Island attracted the attention of society's elite upper-crust; roller skating had entered the realm of roller chic. It wasn't long before rinks began to appear all over America and Europe and to filter down as the favorite pastime of all society classes.

Skating Goes 'Round in Circles

Unfortunately, the popularity of roller skating was to be short-lived. Many rinks were mismanaged in the late 1870s, and most, sad to say, proved boring; once skaters learned the basics, all they could do was roll endlessly around and around—rinks were just too . . . well, dinky for elaborate space-consuming figure, partner, and dance skating. Greedy rink managers prohibited this kind of artistic skating because it subtracted from the numbers of skaters they could send 'round . . . and 'round . . . and 'round. No competition, no music, no instructional programs, it all sent roller skating into bleak obscurity.

A Roller-Coaster Past

Come 1880, the introduction of smoother riding ball-bearing skates by fad-conscious American entrepreneurs created a new roller boom. Using Plimpton's invention as a model, the skate was strapped to the shoe in front and back, with wood, metal, or "deluxe" ivory wheels. These "parlor" skates, as they were termed, came chunkity-chunking out of American machinery by the thousands.

And rink operators had learned their lesson: they built bigger rinks, held exhibitions and competitions, and provided instruction and music. Another notable event during this era was the first six-day roller race, held in Madison Square Garden; the winner wound up skating a total of 1091 miles.

Yet, by the dawn of the Gay Nineties, roller skating would again be pushed gradually into obscurity, this time by another wheeled sport—bicycling. It did not lie dormant though: In 1902, seven thousand people attended the opening of the Chicago Coliseum skating rink; by 1910, eastern businessmen were skating to their offices, and hundreds of rinks had sprouted all over England; by 1912, fads such as acrobatic skating, skating on stilts, barrel jumping, and fancy dance skating were prevalent in both America and Europe.

World War I hurt the sport of roller skating as it hurt most everything else. The large, unobstructed rinks were ready-made supply and factory depots for arms manufacture, and governments took a free hand in requisitioning them.

The Goldie Skating Rink in Sioux City, Iowa, circa 1880 (Sioux City Public Museum).

Not many people returned to the rinks after the war; after all, it was the Roaring Twenties and there were better things to do: flappers and new silent flicks, the Charleston and the new chugging motor car. But for the first time in its history, skating rolled out of the rinks onto something called paved roads. A series of annual roller skating derbies in New York's Central Park drew hundreds of amateur skaters—and crowds of as many as fifty thousand spectators.

The Great Depression Boost

Paradoxically, the pall of the Great Depression provided a needed lift to roller skating, as thousands were forced to sell their rubber motorized wheels and switch to cheaper metal ones. Yet the image of skating rinks in the late twenties and early thirties (which would continue well into the fifties) hovered somewhere between saloons and pool halls—despite the fact that gangsters and punks have not traditionally been known as elegant skaters.

But in the 1937 movie *Shall We Dance,* the elegant team of Fred Astaire and Ginger Rogers glided and tap-skated their way through several Gershwin melodies. And meanwhile the sport was becoming organized. The newly formed Roller Skating Rink Operators Association (RSROA) sanctioned the first national speed skating championship in 1938, and in the following year, the first national figure and dance skating championship. The RSROA was also busy founding an annual professional school where the nation's best instructors could meet and exchange information and standardize teaching procedure.

Another War, Another Decline

World War II brought shortages—shortages of skates and shortages of gasoline to travel to roller rinks. Again, many rinks were converted to defense plants; those that weren't conducted benefits for the Red Cross, the USO, and other organizations.

The slump continued until 1948, when Roller Derby, which had been struggling for more than a decade, took the nation by storm. Its meteoric rise to popularity was accompanied by a steadier growth in competitive skating, but as TV spread so did the waistlines of the American public—roller skating was a

Kenneth Chase, Senior Men's Champion and Charles Peffers, Oakland, California (1942) (Fred Bergin photo).

source of passive amusement (if the bone-rattling antics of Roller Derby would be called "passive"), but the rinks began to deteriorate even more than during the war. Roller rinks in the 1950s and early 60s became synonymous with juvenile delinquency, tough-guy hangouts, and the "wrong kind of girls."

Roller Skating Today

In the late 1960s, the new urethane wheel provided the impetus for a skateboarding craze, and now it is doing the same for roller skating. A new American awareness for health and fitness is seeking new forms of exercise every week—and skating has become the newest.

An early roller derby bone rattler (from the archives of William C. McCoy).

Today, the "punk hangout" image could not be farther from the truth. Rinks are now known as "skating centers," where you're more apt to see the Swiss Family Robinson than Capones, more chance of seeing youngsters hanging in the air than hanging out in dark corners, where modern lighting and sound equipment have transformed skating from obscurity into daily social events.

The RSROA, emerging from its disorganized history of the 1930s, has developed into one of the strongest organizations in amateur athletics. Skate dancing, figures, freestyle, speed, and roller hockey are now standardized, and competitions, though by and large unknown to the general sports public, have been going on for years, both nationally and internationally. In addition, the RSROA sponsors a Proficiency Test Program—

perhaps the best method for beginning skaters to progress in skating skills.

In 1979, roller skating was instituted in the prestigious Pan American Games, and in the 1980s, America along with other countries worldwide, will send its best roller skaters to the Olympic Games.

How far roller skating will go this time is uncertain, but one thing is certain: No one is laughing at roller skating anymore.

PART 2

ROLLER BASICS

3

Those First Baby Rolls

Your first experience on skates will be something like learning to walk on the moon. There will be no gravity, and yet the rink floor or asphalt will be made of banana peels. Leg muscles you never knew existed will be asked to spring to life and translate brain signals sent in a foreign tongue—or the signals will short-circuit altogether before they reach the wheels under your feet.

So if you're trying out skating for the first time, well, it's a good thing you're reading this book—you'll save yourself a great deal of time picking yourself up from the aforementioned surfaces, and at the same time perhaps we can translate some of those brain signals for you.

RENTAL SKATE CHECK-OUT

Let's assume that your sadistic friends have dragged you in chains to the local roller rink. (If your friends are outdoor types, see chapter 13 for additional tips on outdoor skating.) The first order of business (after removing your chains) will be to rent a pair of skates, which, as this book is written, go for a ridiculously cheap $1.00 per hour.

Needless to say, until you've tried skating a few times, it would not be overly wise to go out and buy a $200 pair of Snyder professionals. Unless, of course, you are the type to buy a Cadillac before you learn how to drive, in which case skip right over this section and read chapters 17 through 20 on equipment.

Rental skates, of course, will not be custom-made to your unique individual style or physique any more than a pair of rental bowling shoes, a pool hall cue, or a suit off the rack at Macy's. However, most rinks do maintain their skates in excellent repair; indeed, most buy rugged skates to begin with to withstand the punishment they take day in and day out from people like you.

As compared with outdoor rental skates, rink skates will rarely have wheel "flats"—aptly named imperfections in which one or more of the skate wheels has gone straight. Flats are caused by excessive abrasion, usually on cement, asphalt, or other rough surface, and most rink floors are now made of smooth, epoxy-covered wood. But examine your skates anyway, and if they do have any flats, exchange them.

Your rental skates should be the same size as your shoes. As with any athletic endeavor, wear heavy athletic socks or two pairs of cotton socks to avoid friction and blisters.

• *Shake each skate.* If you hear any rattles, you either have a snake in your skate or a loose wheel or skate assembly.

• Before going out on the floor, *be certain your laces are tied tightly,* not hanging down; a loose shoelace could cause you undesirable entanglements. If your laces are too long, tie them around the top of the boot a few times.

The dreaded wheel flat.

INDOOR SAFETY RULES

You will notice several analogies to automobiles and driving in this book on skating. This is not by chance: Your rink will probably have "House Rules" posted near the rink floor that are much like driving rules—so learn them carefully before entering the flow of traffic to save yourself accidents, tickets, and similar inconveniences:

• When entering the rink floor, the skater already on the floor has the right of way.

• Skate only in the direction of the general traffic (usually counterclockwise). This might seem obvious to an adult, but not so to a child caught up in the excitement and noise of a typical open session.

• Do not speed, push, tailgate, or play any other "tricks," such as "crack the whip," a favorite game among youngsters but very dangerous.

• If by some million-to-one chance you do fall, get up as quickly as possible, preferably facing oncoming traffic.

• Do not stop on the skating floor. (If you must stop, pull over to the wall, as you would pull over to the service lane on a freeway, or hop off at the nearest exit.)

The rink floor seems like the Hollywood Freeway to a novice skater.

• Do not carry combs, pens, or other sharp objects tucked in your skating boots.

• When leaving the skating floor, get over to the right lane, well in advance of your "exit," so as not to cut across the path of other skaters.

If You Bring Your Kids (Or Are One)

We hope we are not scaring you with all this talk of falling, accidents, and rules—pay no heed. Skating is one of the most enjoyable, healthiest, least expensive sports known to man or beast. Further, it is a sport the entire family can learn—and do—together.

So if you're a parent or a kid, here are a couple of pointers to keep in mind:

• Kids are more difficult to see on the rink floor—watch out for them.

• It is probably best to start a child in roller skating classes as soon as possible. Almost all rinks have licensed instructors to provide basic lessons at minimum cost (approximately $4 to $5 per private lesson and only about $1.00 for each group lesson). Most children's classes are run in conjunction with public sessions, which give youngsters valuable practice after the lessons. Many skating centers have graduated classes with awards given after the completion of each course.

While we're on the subject of instruction, Tommy Andrew of the Redwood Roller Rink in Redwood City, California—a rink known internationally for its turn-out of championship competitive skaters—maintains that it takes longer to teach adults and that they usually need much more practice than children. Reasons: Adults have been conditioned longer to movements incompatible to skating, and—perhaps because of this conditioning—they are more fearful. So if you're thinking about lessons for your kids, mull over lessons for yourself also. Qualified personal instruction to accompany what you learn in this book will sculpt you into an expert skater in no time.

Note on Warm-Up

Before any strenuous physical activity you should stretch your muscles. *Warm-up exercises are crucial to avoiding injuries.* If you plan on skating over ten seconds your first time out, you would be wise to read chapter 16, which will give you step-by-step instructions on flexing your muscles during warm-up.

Fresh and Forward

Right at the start, you should recognize that roller skating and walking or running are very different movements. But habit is a difficult rap to beat. A very common mistake for beginning skaters is to continue the walking motion that brought them into the rink. Walking or stepping sends your front skate ahead of your body and throws your weight backward as well, which makes it difficult to transfer your weight and will almost certainly result in your back skate slipping out behind you.

The skating movement is a *slide,* not a step. In fact, in the matter of weight distribution skating is quite the opposite of walking—your weight should be distributed over the middle of the skate, rather than the customary heel-to-toe walking transfer.

Balance. Anatomically speaking, the two heaviest parts of your body are the head and pelvic region; thus, these parts should be aligned in a straight line so that the distribution of

Incorrect Knee Bend   *Correct Knee Bend*

weight is over the middle of the skate. To accomplish this little number, bending your knees is very important. The knees should be used to correct balance problems, rather than breaking at the waist and tilting the pelvis forward and back.

Actually, Margo Lister's position in these photos is in balance. The problem is the precariousness of the balance; the slightest shift will send her lurching forward or back to stay up.

The knees should also be turned out a bit over the top of the feet. Turning them in or allowing them to remain in natural walking position can lead to your skates turning into each other. (*Interesting note:* Roller skating has been used to cure pigeon-toed children.)

Posture. Erect body posture is a tremendous advantage in roller skating. Hold your body straight with a firm back. Developing good posture early will hold you in good stead later on to overcome the forward-lurching tendency when you accelerate or come to a sudden stop. Good posture is also important for breathing to the fullest advantage, that is, to take in the most oxygen. If you become interested in competitive skating (especially the artistic or speed aspects) or want to use skating in a fitness or weight control program, breathing correctly is necessary for aerobic benefits and developing endurance (see chapter 15).

Fear Rears Its Ugly Wheels

The beginning skater's biggest obstacle is fear. If you feel you need an assistant to get your "sea skates," he or she should be positioned at your side (or skate backward in front of you in the case of an experienced teacher). Whatever you do, don't let your helper skate behind you when you are starting out—if you fall, you'll both go down.

Rinks usually have a wall railing, and some instructors use the rail for helping the beginning skater gain balance. The rail has drawbacks, however. The temptation is to hold the rail too long, resulting in the skates sliding out in front of you. The practice of using the rail probably originated in ballet. For now, let it be; if you like it that much, we'll use it later in more advanced stages of training.

Slipping at the rail.

"T" Position

MOVIN' ON

Okay, so now you're on the floor with your body posture erect, your knees bent, your weight over the center of the skates—it's time to get movin'. To start, place your skates in the T position. Then, bringing your right foot parallel to your left, and rocking your weight gently from side to side waddle forward. You will find that your weight shift or lean is propelling you ahead—you're on your way!

This rocking or waddling movement will introduce you to the importance of lean or weight transfer which is integral to all skating maneuvers.

Forward Scissors Movement

The *forward scissors* is another way of learning the mechanics of forward skating motion without lifting your skates from the skating surface. Although the method has gone out of style in recent years, it will be included here to give you valuable experience in using *side-push*—the basic forward skating stroke.

Hints for Beginning Forward Movement

While you're waddling along, try to keep the following in mind:

* *Don't allow your skates to get ahead of your body—or each other.*
* *Focus your mind's attention on your feet, but your vision straight ahead. Bending your head down to see how your feet are doing ruins your posture and your balance.*
* *If you start to lose your balance, apply more pressure to your feet and flex your knees. (Catching your balance by picking up your feet to run won't work.)*
* *Don't lift your skates from the floor. Let them roll in small curves as you lean from side to side.* Coast.
* Relax. *This business is simple if you stay loose.*

The Push

The basic means for forward skating propulsion is a pushing movement of one skate while the other skate simultaneously glides forward.

You are now gliding on your left skate, called the *skating foot* and the right leg is extended behind you off the floor (called the *free* leg).

For correct form the pushing skate should be in contact with the skating surface for as long as possible—until the knee

---

The Forward Scissors

a. Begin with the toes of your skates pointed out at about a 45-degree angle.

b. Using pressure on the inside of your skates, push the skates apart about 12 inches.

c. Now pull the skates in again, at the same time turning into a pigeon-toed stance, until your skates are again a few inches apart.

d. Repeat the movement (out and in) in a smooth pushing and pulling action on the skates.

Forward Scissors

straightens and the leg flows naturally off the floor. At first, the impulse is to "kick" the pushing leg back. Also, to imitate speedster friends, many beginning skaters transfer their weight

The Push

a. Start in the T position. (As you will see, the three "Ss"—standing, starting, and stopping—all begin in some sort of T position.)

b. Bring the right skate close and parallel to the left, and, applying pressure to the inside wheels of the right skate, push down and back with the right skate pointed slightly outward.

c. As you push, transfer your weight (lean) onto the left skate.

d. At the end of your follow-through, begin to bend the knee of your free leg and glide the free skate forward alongside the skating foot.

e. As your free skate touches the floor, begin to push on the inside wheels of your left skate.

f. You are now skating on your right leg, and your left leg has become the free leg.

onto the skating foot too quickly. Both errors result in losing the skate-surface friction necessary for smooth momentum. Remember also that the push should begin on the *inner wheels*, lifting the outer wheels only at the end of a *long stroke*.

Practice exercises. A good practice exercise (that you can make into a game for children) is the "scooter push" that Tommy Andrew teaches at Redwood. Use the push technique

push

free

The Push

Forward Skating Push Stroke

described above but with only one leg (for example, the right leg as the pushing leg) and verbalize the movement: "Push . . . together, push . . . together." See how long you can balance on one skate and still maintain velocity.

The "scooter push" makes you aware of the skating leg, helps you learn to transfer weight from one leg to the other, increases the length of your stroke, and helps to build the shin and quadriceps muscles you will need for skating.

Hints for the Push Stroke

Here are some hints to get you rolling smoothly, effort-lessly, and gracefully:
- *Begin with body erect, knees bent slightly, skates underneath the body and parallel.*
- *Use the entire leg in the pushing movement, not merely from the knee down.*
- *During the push, keep the pelvic area squared (facing forward).*
- *Your arms should be held out, palms facing down-ward, with as little swing as possible. The same holds true for all parts of your body above your waist.*

Having Problems?

Here are some common beginner's faults and how to correct them:

- Skates knocking into each other. You are placing too much weight on the inside of your skates. Shift your weight more over the top of the skates and turn your knees out.
- No momentum. Weight transfer or lean is probably the problem here. Remember to lean onto the skating leg as you push with the other. Also, too much weight over the front two wheels causes the skate to stop suddenly. (We will discuss proper lean in the next chapter.)
- Falling all over the place. You have too much weight on the front part of your skate. Keep your weight behind the toe wheels of the skate. Look into the distance, not down at your feet.

Speaking of falling, one of the most common questions asked by new skaters is *"How the hell do I stop these things?"* Well, the answer is—you can't. Just keep skating until you run into a wall or tree. No, all kidding aside, at this point use a pigeontoed walk-step (similar to the "snowplow" movement in skiing), or a helper or the rail to stop.

There is a full discussion of different ways to stop in chapter 5. If you're concerned about stopping, read that chapter now.

Good luck!

4

Steering Your Wheels

Now that you've got your motor running and you're chugging along, you might ask: How do I steer? Obviously, skates do not have steering wheels so you'll need to find another method for making lefts, rights, heading around curves, and steering around objects and other skaters.

Steering is accomplished, very simply, by leaning or transferring your weight to the left or right. No doubt, you have already swung around the rink or park a few times without telling us, so have guessed how this is done.

The modern roller skate has four wheels that are attached in pairs to two *trucks*. The trucks in turn are attached to the foot *plate* by means of a *pivot* that allows a certain amount of play or *action* and permits the plate to rock from side to side and also allows the trucks to steer on a curve. Thus, as you lean from side to side exerting pressure on your plates, your skate will follow the movement of your body. The curved line of direction that results from body lean is called an *edge* in skating parlance. The depth or arc of the edge depends on the angle or amount of body lean used.

The term *edge* originated in ice skating, that is, the "edge" of the blade, and, in ice figure skating, there are two kinds of edges—inside and outside.

Let's approach the idea of skating edges with a specific example. Suppose you are skating forward on your right skate.

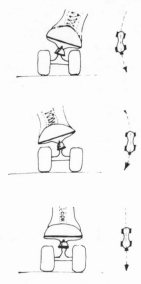

Skating an edge

When the majority of your weight—your lean—is on the outside of your foot, your skate will travel an arc to the right; you are skating what is called in skating lingo a "right-outside-forward" or "ROF" edge. When your lean is on the inner side of the right foot, you are skating a "right-inside-forward" or "RIF" edge.

It's not difficult to see that there are four forward edges: ROF, RIF, LOF, LIF. After we discuss backward skating in the next chapter, you will see that there are also four backward edges: right-outside-back, right-inside-back, left-outside-back, and left-inside-back (ROB, RIB, LOB, LIB).

BODY LEAN

Perhaps the most important aspect of successful skating is proper body lean—so its mastery is essential. For the new skater the process is sometimes difficult for these reasons: When you first learned to walk, your muscles, nervous system, and equilibrium had all they could handle to adjust and hold your body in an upright position. Now your internal system must "unlearn" what it has thought to be correct all these years, that leaning to one side or the other will not result in toppling—as long as there is sufficient forward motion.

The following photos illustrate correct and incorrect body lean. If you are leaning correctly, your head, shoulder, hip, and ankle will be aligned over the middle of the skate aimed toward the direction of travel.

One of the major errors of beginning skaters is "breaking" the lean at the hip (or even skating with no lean at all).

No lean—having your weight evenly distributed over all four wheels—causes the skate to travel in a straight line. This is called skating a *flat* (not to be confused with the dreaded wheel flat), and for technically correct and aesthetically marvelous skating, flats are no-nos.

The modern roller skate (Chicago Roller Skate Co.).

Correct Body Lean

Rockover

Rockover is a term used in roller skating to describe the shift in lean that occurs when you change from one skating foot to the other. Your rockover will be greatly facilitated by bringing the free skate *as close as possible* to the employed skate in preparing for your "takeoff" onto the new edge. This makes a lot of sense. Close takeoffs decrease the amount of shifting, and also increase the length of your side push—which will help you skate smoother and with less effort.

Changing edges with your skates far apart leads to short, choppy, ungraceful side-push—and much less "bounce to the ounce."

AIM THOSE SKATES!

The more edges you skate the more you will realize that a straight line is not the easiest distance between two points. Because curves are skated instead of straight lines, you must aim your skates according to your desired curve depth. On left-outside-forward edges, for example, bring the left skate close

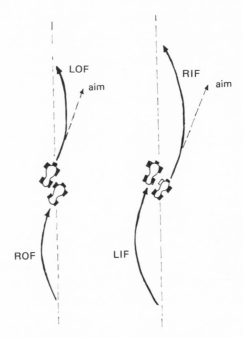

Importance of Aim in Forward Edges

Incorrect Body Lean

and parallel to the right, aiming it to the right of your destination. On inside-forward edges, the newly employed skate should be aimed *slightly diagonally* to the skate finishing the previous edge. A handy rule: lean, aim, and roll.

(For backward skating, as you will see in chapter 6, you must aim the heel rather than the toe according to these same principles.)

Practicing Edges

The novice skater can use the figure circles on the rink floor to practice edges. Using the two-circle configuration (or "figure 8"), start with outside edges, which are simplest for most people. At point *a*, push off onto the outer side of your right skate tracing the circle as far around as you can back to point *a*. Remember that to do a right-outside-forward (ROF) edge, your body lean is toward the center of the circle (*c*). When you return to point *a*, bring the left (free) leg alongside, push onto it with the right, and trace the other circle with a left-outside-forward (LOF) edge, again leaning toward the center.

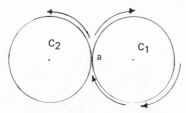

Practicing Edges with Figure Circles

To do an inside edge, reverse your direction around the circles: Trace the first circle counterclockwise on the inner side of your right skate (RIF); the second circle clockwise on the inner side of your left skate. This kind of practice enables you to see an edge graphically and to judge the amount of lean or pressure needed to describe one.

Don't be surprised if you are unable to trace the circle exactly right off the bat or to keep up the momentum to go around the entire circumference. Obviously, circles are deep arcs and anything approaching perfection will only come with practice and increasing the strength of your leg muscles.

No Lean is Just as Bad

Many people find inside edges more difficult because of the stress on the knee from inside pressure on the skate. Also, skating an inside edge requires distributing the body weight over the arch rather than the "meatier" part of the foot. (And using rental skates does not make the task any easier; the age of the cushions vary, as does the action of the trucks.)

Believe it or not, you have just begun your first course in figure roller skating. If you glance at the ROF-LOF circle eight in chapter 9, you'll get an idea whether you've been skating edges properly. (Indeed, many teachers view figure skating as an excellent means of teaching edge control so vital to freestyle skating.) If by some miracle you have been able to do the practice exercises described above perfectly, you have skated figures 1 and 2 used in USAC figure skating competition.

Hints for Practicing Edge Control

• *Shift your weight—not your body. The pelvic area remains over the skate that is describing the edge, rather than jutting out over the floor.*
• *Keep the knee of your skating leg flexed. This will help a great deal with your lean and momentum.*

5

Applying the Brakes

Aside from falling, smacking into something, or plain old running out of momentum, there are two different methods for stopping on skates: the T stop and the toe-stop stop.

T-STOP

The principle behind the T-stop method is that wheels will not roll sideways. Very scientific.

Assume you are skating forward, with your left leg the skating leg and the right leg free. To stop, simply bring the right skate up to the heel of the left at a 90-degree angle, which is merely a return to the T starting position you learned in chapter 3, and gradually lower it to the floor. Slowly transfer your weight onto the right skate; the friction of the right skate on the floor acts as the brake.

Remember, as with any vehicle, the skating stop is a *gradual* one, and you don't want to jam on your skating brakes any more than you would in your car. An analogy that children will readily grasp is the bicycle brake. When riding a bicycle, you don't want to slam on the brakes—the bicycle will stop, but you won't. Same thing on skates: your lower body will stop, but the top part is going to lurch forward.

T-Stop

Hints on the T-Stop

- *Keep the left knee bent.*
- Place down all four wheels of the right skate. *A common error is to allow the skate to trail with only the two inside wheels touching the skating surface. To practice keeping eight wheels on the ground, place the outside wheels down first.*
- Resist tendency to lean forward. *Keep weight over the skating leg until the trailing leg has landed and you will slowly "drag" to a halt.*
- Do not let the hips or right shoulder flare out. *For good skating form, make sure they are squared.*

(You can use either the right or left leg to stop by the way; just reverse the directions given above.)

TOE-STOP STOP

When doing simple forward skating, the toe-stops on your skates are about as useful as an umbrella in the desert. Rather they are on your skates as a security measure, much like the emergency brake in your car, as a method of stopping backward skating (see chapter 6), and to protect your boots. (On old-style skates with no toe stops, the toe of the boot would curl up with wear.)

However, if you would like to give your toe stops a whirl, bring the free leg behind the skating leg, touch the floor with your toe-stop of the trailing skate, and exert pressure until you stop. Whatever, you do, don't use the toe stop of your skating foot unless absolutely necessary—you'll surely pitch over into a fall.

FALLING FOR YOU

Speaking of falling, there are certain ways of falling that will greatly reduce your chances of injury. When you do feel yourself being overcome by gravity, so to speak, the number one

Toe-Stop Stop

rule is *relax*. Most of us have been provided with ample natural padding, which will absorb the shock waves of any terra-posterial collision.

Toppling forward is another story. The first impulse is to stick out your arms—try to resist this impulse. Instead, roll over onto the fleshier parts of your arms, shoulders, and upper torso. And *relax*.

6

In Reverse: Rolling Backwards

Okay, wild and crazy skaters, ready for some fancy maneuvers? The techniques of backward skating are, amazingly enough, almost exactly the same as forward skating—except that you will be facing in the opposite direction.

One important note before we start: Make sure you have mastered the balance, body lean, and side-pressure push stroke of forward skating before you begin to skate backward.

The similarities to forward skating:

1. Weight distribution is over the forward part of the skate;
2. Propulsion is acquired from *pushing* one skate then the other, and from the mechanics of body lean;
3. The skating knee is bent.

BACKWARD SCISSORS

To get you started rolling backwards, the scissors movement—actually the forward scissors described in chapter 3 *in reverse*—is the quickest way to gain the "feel" and the confidence for skating backward. The reason many people do not pick up backward skating right away is simply the lack of experience in *walking* backward. The unfamiliar motions plus not being able to see what's behind you often translate into fear and muscle tension, which in turn further inhibit coordination.

Enlisting the aid of a friend to skate forward as you skate backward usually hastens the entire process.

Using the "buddy system" for backward skating

The Backward Scissors

a. The starting position for the backward scissors is a slightly pigeon-toed stance, but the skater should obey all the elements of proper forward skating technique (such as erect posture, flexed knees, weight over middle of skate, and so on).

b. Exert pressure on the inside wheels (especially the inside front wheels). You will feel the skates begin to flare out and backward as you push.

c. When your skates are twelve to sixteen inches apart (no farther than shoulder-width), begin to turn the heels back in while still pushing on the inside of the skates.

d. When your heels are within a few inches of each other, turn them out again and repeat the push in a smooth and continuous movement.

Your skates will travel a pattern like this:

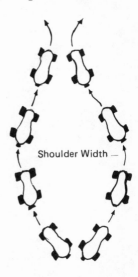

Backward scissors pattern

Hints for the Backward Scissors

• *Don't let the skates knock together. If this happens, you lose all velocity. You'll be doing something called stationary skating.*

• *Don't allow skates to scissors out too far. More than twelve to sixteen inches usually results in a loss of·control; that is, it becomes difficult to pull the skates back in and you lose momentum.*

• *Involved with new muscle coordination for the first time, you'll want to glance down at your skates to see how you're doing. Bending the head forward to take a peek leads to jutting out the posterior to compensate for the imbalance. Remember, as in forward skating, keep good posture; your eyes should be peering straight ahead (except for a glance or two behind you to see what's coming up).*

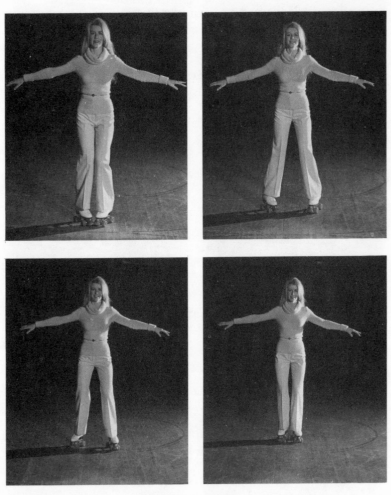

Backward Scissors

The backward scissors, indeed all backward skating technique will seem to come to you as if in a dream, almost as much in spite of your practice as because of it. Once you do master it, however, you'll find it exciting—not to mention a great strengthener of thigh muscles.

Incorrect Posture

BACKWARD SKATING

The basic backward skating stroke is very similar to the "side-push" forward stroke. To begin, gain momentum with the backward scissors movement you just learned. Then, with the same side-push off the inside wheels you learned for forward skating, push *forward* with the right skate, gliding back on your left. (Thus, your right leg becomes the free leg and should be in front of you.) Then, bring back the right skate until it is parallel and close to the left, preparing to push off with the left. (When you push off with the left skate, glance over your right shoulder to see what's in back of you.)

To stop when skating backwards is quite elementary: As you bring your free leg back to a parallel position to the skating leg, place the toe stop on the floor, exert slight pressure, and gradually come to a full stop.

Backward Push

Using toe-stops in backward skating

The Backward Edge

In chapter 4 we discussed the importance of good posture, proper body lean, close takeoffs, aiming the skates, bending the knees, keeping the weight over the middle of the skate. All of these elements apply to backward skating as well.

Hints for Backward Skating

• *Hold body erect. Do not get into a crouch or sitting posture.*

• *Aiming. The heel is aimed rather than the toe: close and parallel for outside backward edges.*

• *Straighten your free leg in front of you as the weight is shifted to the skating leg. Body lean is* into *the center of the arc you create.*

7

Shifting Gears: Turn, Turn, Turn

Now that you're expert at skating forward and backward, you'll want to know how to make the transition between the two. The transition is accomplished by means of turns. Basically, there are two kinds of turns: two-foot turns and one-foot turns.

TWO-FOOT TURNS

Two-foot turns are all different variations of the Mohawk, in which both skates are employed simultaneously in the transition. Because the one-foot turns employ one skate, the mechanism of turning is a shift of lean and pressure during the forward-to-backward maneuver.

Open Mohawk Turn

Say you are skating around the rink (forward) in a typical counterclockwise direction and want to razzle-dazzle everyone present by switching to backward skating. You'll want to try the least complicated turn, the *Mohawk,* which is done as follows:

a. From a left-outside forward (LOF) edge, take off to a right-inside-forward (RIF) edge. Begin to rotate your shoulders to the left (center of the rink) and your left free leg in the same direction. Make sure at this point that you are still balanced solidly over the right skate.

b. Bringing the left skate close to the floor and its heel close

57

to the heel of the right skate, open your body position fully so that you are facing the center of the floor.

c. Now, lower the left skate to the floor so that all four wheels touch. At this point, both skates are on the floor—one aimed forward the other backward, but both following the same curve. (This position, with both skates in alignment, toes pointing in opposite directions, is a "spread eagle" position. (The real spread eagle entails much wider distance between skates, as shown below.) All two-foot turns use some variation of the

A

B

C

Open Mohawk Turn

spread eagle for the transition from forward-to-backward or backward-to-forward skating.) Now, your body weight should be distributed equally over both skates.

    d. Immediately, transfer your weight onto the left skate.

    e. Simultaneously lift your right skate off the floor (onto an LIB edge).

    f. Push off with the left foot onto the right, transferring your weight to the right skate and—*voila!* You are skating backward (ROB)!

D

E

F

Open Mohawk Turn

Spread Eagle Position

Needless to say, the actual turn should take much less time than it takes to read about it.

In roller skating, movements are often diagrammed to illustrate the edge sequence and direction. The Mohawk turn would be diagrammed as shown below, the numbers corresponding roughly to the steps of instruction above.

Examining the diagram, you can see that the Mohawk is used to turn from a forward edge to the same backward edge on the other skate, thus continuing the same curve of direction. There are three other possible combinations of edges other than the RIF-LIB combination shown above: LIF-RIB, ROF-LOB, LOF-ROB.

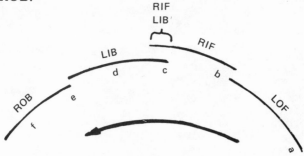

Mohawk turn

Common Errors

• *Inability to align skates.* By far the most prevalent error of first-time Mohawk-turners, the only way to correct it is through constant practice and rail exercises. Grasp the rail or a door-knob in your own home (on skates or off) with the heels of your skates or shoes together against the wall. Slowly, lean back until you feel pressure on the shin and thigh muscles; hold for thirty seconds; repeat. In chapters 15 and 16, there are more exercises you can do to increase the flexibility and strength of the muscles used in skating.

• *Dropping left shoulder.* Many people have the tendency to drop the left shoulder when the left skate is placed on the floor. This, along with tilting the pelvis out and the hips in, will make your arc too deep. A good method of keeping the left shoulder up is to skate with the arms out at shoulder height.

• *Inability to make the forward-backward transition.* The causes are probably twofold: (1) Be certain to lift the right skate *up* off the floor, rather than sliding it off or allowing it to jostle on the floor; (2) Body lean is important in the transition. Because you are skating inside edges during the transition, be certain your body lean is in over your skates. Also, the rotation of the shoulders must be smooth and continuous. If you are still having trouble with the turn, it is probably because of the fear factor; go back to the chapter on backward skating and practice until skating backward is as automatic for you as skating forward.

Backward to Forward Mohawk Turn

Now, continuing along in the rink or at the park, assume you're becoming a little bored with backward skating and wish to "re-turn" to forward skating.

a. You're on a right-outside-back edge (the last step of the Mohawk) and want to continue your curve of direction.

b. First, rotate the torso to the left, and swing your (left) free leg to the left also so that the heel is at the right instep and the toe pointed out at about 90 degrees.

c. As you take off on your left skate (LOF), shift your weight from right to left. (Many skaters will prepare for this new edge by first unbending the right knee just before takeoff.)

d. Bring right skate forward close and parallel to the left ready for the next stroke.

Closed Mohawk Turn

Like the open Mohawk turn, the closed Mohawk is a half-turn from a forward edge to a similar backward edge—or vice versa.

a. The turn begins on an LOF edge.

b. Bring the instep of the right skate behind the left heel. Keep the knee of the right skate bent slightly.

c. Straightening the right knee, drop the right skate to the floor, simultaneously lifting the left and preparing for the next edge. You are now skating backward (ROB); the turn is completed.

Closed Mohawk Turn

The differences between the open and closed Mohawk in terms of foot placement are shown below:

Difference Between Open and Closed Mohawk

Mohawk Pointers

• *Keep hips squared. Over-rotating the body during the change of edges inevitably leads to loss of balance and flop-flop fizz-fizz.*

• *Hold left body lean well into the change of edge. This will also help your balance.*

Chocktaw Turn

A Chocktaw is another type of two-foot turn actually a variation of the Mohawk. Like the Mohawk, the result is a 180-degree half-turn; the difference is that the half-turn is from a forward edge to the *opposite* backward edge. What this means is that the curve of direction is in the form of an "S."

a. Begin the Chocktaw on a left-outside-forward (LOF) edge.

b. Bring the right skate behind the left so that the instep of the right skate is close to the heel of the left (that is, pointing backward).

c. Place the right skate on the skating surface (skating a right-inside-backward (RIB) edge, and lift the left. The rotation of the upper body should be smooth and continuous. You are now skating backwards, preparing for your next edge on the left foot.

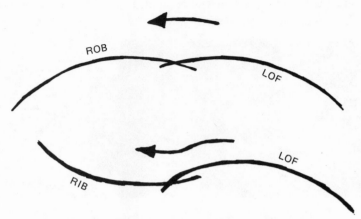

Comparison of Chocktaw and Closed Mohawk Turns

ONE FOOT TURNS

Changing the direction of your skates utilizing only one skate is called (obviously enough) a one foot turn. One foot turns also go under the alias of "three turns" (not so obviously enough) because of the shape of the turn. A three turn looks something like the diagram below. To accomplish the movement, the body is rotated either in the direction of the edge or in the opposite direction while the front wheels of one skate are used as a pivot.

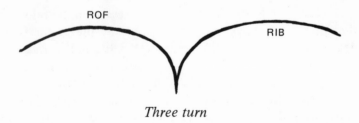

Three turn

To illustrate, Margo Lister does a ROF-RIB three turn; the rotation of the body is in the same direction (clockwise) as the original edge.

a. Skate a good strong outside edge. (This means getting a good push from your free skate to start and maintaining good body lean into the edge.) The free leg should be well behind the

One-Foot (Three) Turn

employed skate, and you should have an "open hip" to provide the "rubber-band snap" necessary to make the turn.

b. Just before the point of the turn (called the *cusp* in skating parlance), transfer your weight from the outside to the inside of your skate using the front wheels as a pivot and rotating the upper part of the body. Danny MacNiece, life member of the Society of Roller Skating Teachers of American (SRSTA), uses

One-Foot Turn Pointers

• *Keep free leg firm and well-extended behind employed skate.*

• *When entering the cusp of the turn, bend your skating knee; do not change your body lean or straighten up so that your weight shifts to the back portion of the skate.*

• *Do not "kick" the free leg during the turn; the three turn uses* rotation, *not swing.*

• *Check the "snap" of the lower body with the shoulders and arms to counterbalance.*

Outdoor Disco in Central Park

the analogy of driving into your garage and then backing out in the same direction.

c. You are now skating backward—in this case on an inside edge.

Brackets, Rockers, and Counters

One foot turns may be categorized according to the edges employed and the direction of body rotation. A *bracket* is a one-foot turn from a forward edge to the opposite backward edge (or vice versa), and the rotation of the body is against the original edge.

A *rocker* is a one-foot turn from a forward edge to a similar backward edge (or vice versa) and rotation is in the same direction as the original edge.

A *counter* is a one-foot turn from a forward edge to a similar backward edge (or vice versa); rotation of the turn is against (counter to) the direction of the original edge.

A NOTE ON PSYCHOLOGY:

At this point in your skating career it is a good practice to get a clear mental image of each movement you intend to do. This means each part of the turn: position of arms, body lean, rotation, free leg placement, etcetera.

If you run through in your mind each part of the turn—you'll find the actual turn much less difficult.

PART 3

DIFFERENT STROKES
FOR
DIFFERENT FOLKS

8

Floating Together: Dance Skating, Free Dance, Roller Disco

Dancing and skating are as naturally suited to one another as Fred Astaire and Ginger Rogers. Dancing on skates, you'll be so "light on your feet," your feet won't even touch the floor.

As with many other aspects of roller skating, roller dance evolved from ice dance. From the forceful, leaned-into strokes of ice dance developed the progressive parallel stroking and upright posture more suited to the glide of the roller skate.

Traditional roller dances may be categorized into three groups: beginning, intermediate, and advanced. The RSROA Dance Proficiency Tests (Bronze, Silver, and Gold) progress through these dances on something called a "proficiency ladder." Like the other RSROA proficiency tests, the dance tests are not competitive nor even necessary for entering competitions. However, they are extremely useful as "guides" for the skater to test for skills achievement. (Write the RSROA, 7700 "A" Street, Lincoln, Nebraska 68510, for further information on RSROA proficiency tests, or contact your local rink.) The candidate usually skates with a partner who has already passed the test or an instructor; sometimes, both members of the team take the test simultaneously, but this is the exception rather than the rule.

To be eligible for the next highest rung, the skater must pass all previous tests in the series. Successfully passing the two dances discussed here—the Progressive Tango and the Glide

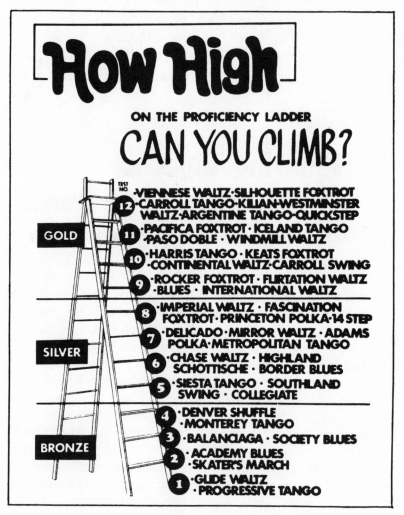

RSROA Dance Proficiency Ladder

Waltz—would qualify the skater for the First Bronze award, and allow the team to move up to the more complicated dances that occupy the rungs of the other Bronze tests.

All dances in the RSROA proficiency test ladder are standardized—if you're a Bronze dance skater from Indianapolis, for example, and happen to find yourself in Sioux Falls, you could go to the Sioux Falls Skatarama, find a partner, and immediately dance the Denver Shuffle—which is pretty handy info for traveling roller skate gigolos.

Starting Positions

The five basic starting positions—there are also variations of these—are shown below. The partners' hand and arm grasp should be firm yet prepared to change as the edges and strokes change. Obviously, the objective of the dancers should be symmetry and synchronization throughout the dance.

Dance Starting Positions

Dance Starting Positions

Form Notes

- Posture should be erect, eyes level.
- Dance should be performed with ease, all stiff or angular movements avoided.
- Good footwork is essential.

PROGRESSIVE TANGO

Although the Glide Waltz is commonly the first dance taught, we'll begin with the Progressive Tango. As Tommy Andrew points out, tango music has a 100-beat-per minute tempo, as opposed to the 108-beat waltz music; the more lilting melodies of the waltz have contributed to the misconception that it is a "slower" dance. Besides, the Tango is more exciting than the Waltz.

The Progressive Tango is started about midway down the straightaway of the rink floor in side or cross-arm position. Most dances begin with four opening or "power" steps: in this case a LOF-RIF-LOF-RIF sequence that will take you toward the wall or barrier (though body lean is toward the left or center of the rink). Each opening step is held for two beats of the music.

1. You are now nearing the corner, prepared for the *corner steps* or *corner sequence*. Bring both feet parallel and skate an LOF edge for one beat.

2. Skate an RIF for one beat.

3. The LOF third step is held for two beats.

4. Perform a *front crossover* with the right foot (XF-RIF), and hold it for two beats. This is the last step in the corner sequence; you should be somewhere around the back-middle of the floor tracing the same counterclockwise arc. Most rinks are large enough to do the corner sequence twice at each end of the floor, so that the corner steps are immediately repeated.

The *straightaway steps* are a series of three steps, beginning with an LOF and an RIF for one beat each (the same two steps as the corner sequence). The third straightaway step is skated on the left foot—half on the outside edge, half on the inside (this change of edge is abbreviated LOIF)—for a total of six beats. On the third beat of this LOIF, bring the right leg forward from its trailing position, extend it fully, touching the

The Crossover Step

Front Toe Point

outside-front wheel lightly to the floor in front of the right foot. (This is known as a *front toe point*, abbreviated FTP.) During the second three beats of the LOIF, rockover is to the right, and the right leg is extended back to the trailing position, the front inside wheel touching the floor lightly on the fifth beat of music (known as a *back toe point*, or BTP).

You are now on the center of the floor again, prepared for another straightaway sequence. This one also has three steps similar to the first but on opposite feet—ROF and LIF for one beat each, then a six-beat ROIF curving to the skater's right (toward the barrier) with a front and back toe point with the left skate.

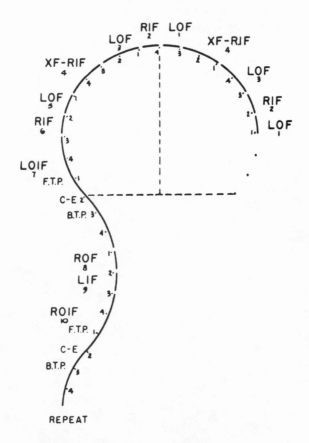

Progressive Tango (United States Amateur Confederation of Roller Skating)

Dance Diagrams

The Progressive Tango (indeed all patterned roller dancing) may be diagrammed, as shown below. The abbreviations you know already. The curved dash line represents the tracing of the dance around the rink floor, the length of each dash corresponding to the length of each stroke and number of beats that the stroke is held. The bulges out to the left and right are called *barrier lobes*; the inward bulges, *center lobes*.

Progressive Tango Pointers

There are three new movements in this dance—crossovers, changes of edge in the middle of a stroke, and toe points.

- Crossovers. *To perform this maneuver properly, the heel wheels of the crossover skate should be aligned with the toe wheels of the back skate. Bending the knee of the skating leg as you cross it will make this movement much easier. Also, try to keep the skates parallel; many beginning skate dancers walk slightly bowlegged and so allow the crossover foot to "angle back" and hit the back skate. The crossover is a four-wheel change; all four wheels should be on the floor.*

- Mid-stroke change of edge (LOIF). *On the first beat of this six beat stroke you should bend your skating knee; on the second beat begin to rise up to bring your free leg forward on beat three; on beat four rock over to the inside edge and bring your free leg back to touch on beat five.*

- Toe points. *The toe points are aided by bending the skating knee and shifting weight forward slightly. The toe should be pointed slightly outward.*

GLIDE WALTZ

Like the Progressive Tango, the Glide Waltz is started about midway down the straightaway in either the side or crossed-arm position. The four opening steps are also the same, except that

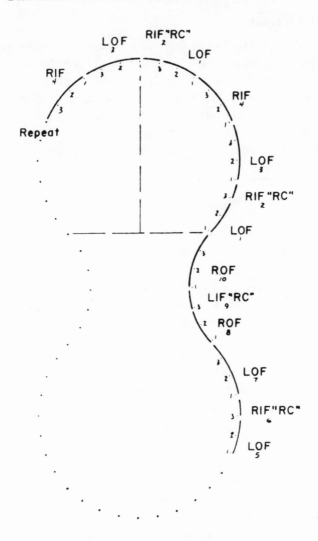

*Glide Waltz (United States Amateur
Confederation of Roller Skating)*

each is held for three beats of music rather than two. The corner steps go as follows:

1. Hold an LOF for two beats.

2. Perform raised *chasse* (pronounced shah-say) for one beat. A chasse is done simply by raising one skate (in this case the left) from the floor about one inch alongside the other skate.

Chasse Step   *Good Waltz Form*

3. Hold an LOF for three beats.
4. Hold an RIF for three beats.

The corner sequence is repeated. The straightaway steps:

5. An LOF for two beats.
6. An RIF chasse for one beat.
7. An LOF for three beats.

You will notice these are the same as the first three steps of the opening sequence.)

Steps 8, 9, and 10 are the same as 5, 6, and 7—except on opposite feet (ROF, LIF chasse, ROF). The steps will take you in toward the center and then out again.

FREE DANCE

Since World War II, free dance has gradually but continually worked its way into the roller competitive arena. Dancing in world ice skating competitions had a profound impact at first: Influenced by the ice skaters' bent-forward posture, roller dance teams adopted many forceful ice techniques. An

Free Dance Originality . . .

. . . and Virtuosity

American member of the RSROA, Perry Rawson, realizing that roller skating should have its own style more suited to wheels and wood floors, introduced a smoother, more upright style that the team of Clifford Schattenkirk and Bettie Jennings used to win the American Senior Dance Championship in 1947.

The "American" style did not catch on worldwide for many years, but once it did, acceptance was complete. In 1976, American free-dance teams placed one, two, three in the World Championships in Rome, Italy.

Free dance is similar to pairs freestyle (see chapter 10), except that no overhead lifts are allowed and the partners must be in contact at all time. Although free dance routines are somewhat more standardized than pairs, the movements, choice of music (usually at least three different types in different rhythms to show the team's versatility), and interpretation of music are entirely up to the teams themselves. The accompanying photos show the grace, coordination, and precision that have become common in roller dance choreography.

Disco Ladiequins (Bob Kingsbook photo).

SHAKE YOUR BOOTY: ROLLER DISCO

Whatever your opinion of today's popular music, the invasion of "disco" music into rinks (and the skate's invasion into discos) is unmistakable. During open rink sessions, disco-brand music vibrates from the sound systems as much as any other type of music; there is somehow an affinity between the pulsating disco beat and the rhythmic stroking and movement of roller skating.

Disco Deluge has not exactly been discouraged by rink operators, who have installed multicolored lights, strobes, and complex sound systems to cater to the tastes of their younger skaters. Moreover, disco-beat and movement has spread into the free style and free-dance routines of competitive skating.

There are really two different types of roller disco: dancing to disco on skates in place, as you would on your feet, and roller disco dancing at full speed (called "rexing" or "freaking"). The former type doesn't have a heckuva lot to do with skating except for some rarely used spins and lifts. Most of the well-known disco dances were created for feet, so doing them to form—on skates—amounts to little more than boogieing on toe stops, which is about as comfortable and aesthetically pleasing as doing a ballet on stilts.

Rexing, however, is a different story, fitting together much more easily with the skating essence: long glides on wheels, creative choreography, and multidirectional movement over a large area.

Here is Sally R. Sommer, writing in the New York *Village Voice*, after a visit to the Empire Rollerdome, perhaps the nation's capitol of roller disco:

> The astonishing thing about hardcore (disco) skaters is their sweetness of disposition, generosity of feeling, their openness. I had imagined that skaters would be tough, fast—exciting, yes—but with a kind of fierceness no doubt influenced by visions of roller derby. I was totally unprepared for the poetry of their body movements and the eloquence of their special language about skating.

Gold Skates Classic.

9

Figure It Out

The art of figure skating originated on the ice: Skaters cut all kinds of complex geometric patterns on the ice and judges awarded prizes for originality and the "cleanness" of the cut pattern. From this "open canvas" beginning evolved the "school figures"—exact, rigidly defined patterns that are used both in ice and roller figure skating.

Today, ice figure skating is given little media attention. It is the part *Wide World of Sports* omits from its coverage, the part "done earlier this morning." Thus, many roller skaters interested in the competitive side of skating recklessly overlook figure skating—recklessly because the control and discipline gained from the art are crucial to the more "exciting" branches of artistic skating, such as free style, pairs, and free dance.

ROLLER FIGURES

In roller figure skating, the patterns that the skaters must trace are painted one-half to three-quarter inches wide on the rink floor. These patterns can be categorized into three types: *figure eights, serpentines,* and *loops.*

The figure (or circle) eight is actually formed by two circles of equal diameter (either five or six meters) that are tangent at one

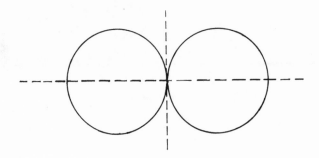

Figure Eight

point. The diagram below illustrates the different figures and the different reference points you will need to know to skate the figures. The dotted lines are called *axes*: Line A is the *long axis*, which divides the circle into four equal parts, by passing through the center of both circles, the point of tangency, and the opposite ends of both circles. Line B is called the *short* or *transverse* axis, which intersects the long axis at a right angle and also passes through the point of tangency.

This book cannot discuss all the school figures skated on these configurations for RSROA proficiency tests and USAC competitions, so we will choose a few that are representative of the patterns, edges, and turns used in figure skating.

ROF-LOF Circle Eight

For most people the ROF-LOF Circle Eight is the easiest figure to master because the skating is done on the outer, meatier, and usually stronger part of the foot.

a. The take-off begins from a stationary position on the intersection of the long and short axis. (Actually, in RSROA proficiency tests, rolling starts are permitted on this figure. These must consist of two forward strokes starting on the short axis.) For the ROF-LOF figure, the two front wheels of the right skate are over the long axis; the left skate is placed behind the right in a "push" position. The arms are extended out to the side (or forward over the trace of the circle), with the hands palms down and about waist high.

A

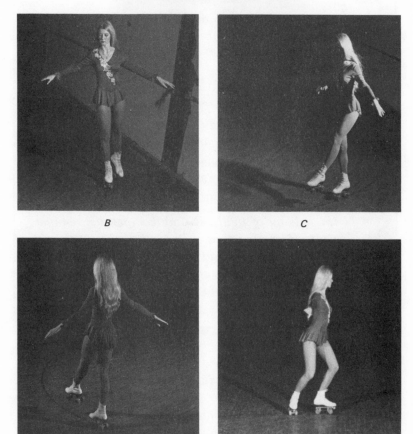

B

C

D

E

ROF-LOF Circle Eight

b. Push with the left skate, which will remain behind you and close to the floor as the free leg, and roll around the circle to your right on the outer edge of your right skate (ROF edge).

c. About one-half around the circle, bring the left leg forward . . .

d. And continue to roll in this position, left foot forward.

e. Returning to the start, push off onto the left leg, and trace the second circle to the left on the LOF edge.

Figure Pointers

• *On the take-off, do not lunge forward. The edge should be started purely, that is, with no flats or subcurves. On the initial take-off (sometimes referred to as the* strike-off *or* start), *there is a "strike zone—one skate length—that the skater must stay within.*

• *Do not lean forward. The skater should travel the circles with a steady pace; any pulling or steering to gain momentum is considered poor form.*

• *Maintain proper balance. If you can't, momentum and pace will be difficult to achieve. Small movements of the knee are sufficient to shift balance and lean.*

• *In the judging of figure skating competition, emphasis is given to form as well as the actual tracing of the circles. Remember that the head should be held erect. Resist the tendency to glance down at the circle; looking ahead at the circle using the front hand as a "tracing guide" will be all you need.*

RIF-LIF Circle Eight

The inside edges are used for this figure—forward on the right for the first circle, forward on the left for the second. The inside forward edge start is slightly different from the outside: (1) The heel of the left (pushing) skate starts near the *instep* of the right skate, and (2) the left shoulder is forward—instead of the right—to aid the balancing on the inside of the right foot.

Rotary Push for Backward Circle Eight

ROB-LOB Circle Eight

The first backward figure will take a good bit of your time, patience, and practice. Make sure you have mastered the basic backward skating stroke discussed in chapter 6 before beginning this figure.

The start for the outside back figure is known as the *rotary push* start. The idea behind this kind of start being that you will need power of a body windup to maintain the one edge throughout an entire circle:

Lift the right foot off the floor and at the same time rotate it inward as the arms and upper body follow the rotation into a "coiling position." Now, when your left leg pushes off, you will have the necessary power.

Serpentine Figures

Add one more circle tangentially to your figure eight and you've got a serpentine. As you can see, because of the extra circle, there is an extra short axis. Also, the point at which the long axis intersects the outside circle is called the *apex*, important because this is where all turns—brackets, rockers, and counters both into and out of the circles—take place.

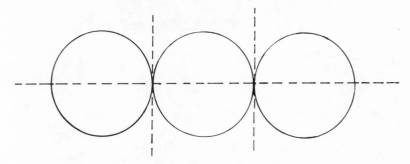

Serpentine Figure

Loop Figures

Most skaters rate loops as the most difficult figures to master mainly because of the configuration itself. The loop is actually elliptical in shape—but only one-third the size of the circle. This makes balancing and maintaining one edge throughout the circle and the loop a very delicate proposition indeed, because body rotation must be quicker, and the pacing of the entire figure must be altered to accommodate the shift.

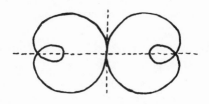

Loop Figure

10

Forging a Freestyle: Jumps, Spins, and Fancy Footwork

For the most part, freestyle skating is what its name implies. To quote from the RSROA's *Roller Free Skating* competition manual:

> The basic movements on a free skating routine consist of jumps, spins, and footwork, which are blended in harmony with the skater's choice of music. Free skating permits complete freedom as to the style, content, and music used in the composition. Skaters are not restrained by prescribed routines or patterns as exist in Figure and Dance skating.

Although you are not restrained by the prescribed routines of dance skating, the rhythm and footwork you acquired from it are essential. No more school figures to trace, but edge control and balance remain crucial.

Jim Pollard, operator of the Redwood Roller Rink and skating professional for many years, emphasizes the importance of good footwork. "It's impossible to be a jumper or a spinner if you can't skate," he affirms in the RSROA's *Skate* magazine. "A skater has to first fundamentally learn to roller skate. I'm a serious believer that the skater first learns to skate, dance, do figures, *then* he learns freestyle. . . . If you can't control your skates, how can you get in the air?"

Classic freestyle skating comes in two sizes: singles and pairs. In either case, the freestyle program should be a *composition* of elements—jumps, spins, and footwork—that is in artistic harmony with the accompanying music.

The skater interested in freestyle skating should get a good licensed skating teacher to complement the instructional material in this book.

JUMPS

Thus far, your skating education has been planar, that is, at least one skate on the floor at all times. Now, we will enter a new dimension—the air—where what you do and how you do it will determine whether you land on your skates or your anatomy.

Two-foot Practice for Jumping

Jumps are differentiated according to (1) the edges used for take-off and landing, (2) the direction of body rotation (clockwise or counterclockwise), and (3) the number of turns in the air—½, ¾, 1, 1½, or 2. A ½-turn jump, for example, means that the body has turned 180 degrees, from forward to backward (or vice versa). In general, the greater the number of turns in the air, the greater the difficulty of the jump.

For our purposes, jumps may be broken down into two categories: one-foot jumps, and toe-assisted jumps (in which you'll finally get to use those toe-stops for something besides looks).

One-Foot Jumps

First, let's see what the weather is like in the air. From a standing start, jump in the air a few times with your skates on to get a feel for the spring needed for take-off and the difficulties involved in maintaining your balance in landing. Remember, you are carrying about fifteen pounds more than usual. Keep your feet parallel and your knees bent on take-off and landing.

Then, practice turning in the air as you jump, rotating your body in one direction or the other. The simplest one-foot jumps are *hops* and *leaps* because they require no turns in the air. In either case, the landing foot may be the same as the takeoff foot or may be the other foot.

Bunny Hop

The bunny hop is the first jump for a beginner. You may use either the right or left skate, outside or inside edge, or flat, depending on your intended direction.

The free leg is swung forward on takeoff. At landing, the toe of the free leg touches the floor alongside and in front of the landing foot.

Bunny Hop

Bunny Hop

Forward Leap

The forward leap is done from a left forward edge to a right forward edge (or vice versa), or on a flat as in the bunny hop. The jump is usually done in a *split position* (legs extended in opposite directions) at the start but may also be done in a *stag position* (one leg bent under the body).

Waltz Jump

The first jump employing body rotation, it is a ½ turn in the air. The skater takes off from an LOF edge, with the free leg swung in the air for lift power. In the photos below, Steve Lister rotates counterclockwise, but if the takeoff is from the ROF edge, rotation is clockwise. Landing is on the ROB edge with the free leg in "landing position" (extended straight back).

Waltz Jump

Waltz Jump

TOE-ASSISTED JUMPS

Half Mapes

The half mapes is a half turn that takes off backwards and lands forwards. The direction of rotation is with the edge. The takeoff is assisted by the toe stop of the free skate. The skater lands on the same foot as the takeoff.

Half Mapes Jump

FULL-TURN JUMPS

Salchow

The Salchow is a full turn jump—from a backward edge to a backward edge on the opposite foot. Before many jumps that take off from a backward edge, the skater will insert a preparatory turn to "set up" the jump from the proper edge. The

Half Mapes Jump

preparatory turn should blend with the jump and the overall composition of the routine. For the Salchow the turn is usually the LOF-LIB three turn or the RIF-LIB Mohawk—both of which you have already learned.

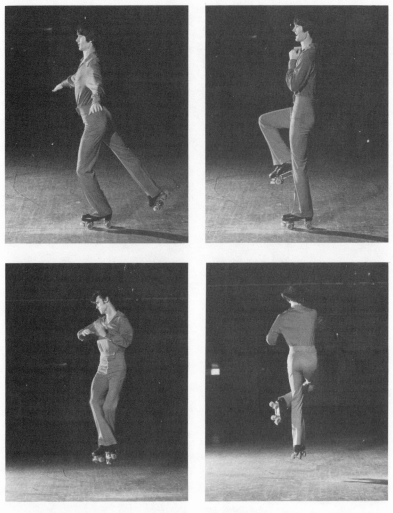

Salchow Jump

Once on the LIB edge, take off on the left arch, swinging your right leg counterclockwise. On the right outside back landing, the left leg is swung back into landing position.

LIB   ROB

Salchow Jump

Salchow Jump

Flip

The flip jump is very similar to the Salchow, except that the toe stop of the free skate assists in takeoff.

Axel

The axel is an advanced jump—as are all 1½ turn jumps. The skater does 1½ revolutions in the air—taking off from a forward edge (LOF or ROF) and landing on a backward edge (ROB or LOB).

After you do one of these you'll be well on your way to a career in competitive skating.

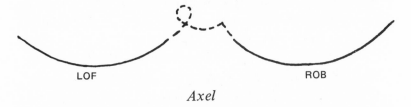

LOF   ROB

Axel

These are only a few of the jumps possible on roller skates. With all the take-offs, preparatory turns, in-air positions, and landings, the possibilities are virtually limitless. It should be stressed, however, that you obtain the instruction of a licensed skating teacher before attempting any of the jumps illustrated.

JUMPING TECHNIQUE

Takeoff. Principles of acrobatics and physics tell us that the technique you use in takeoff determines, to one extent or another, your flight and landing. In other words, "how you go up is gonna be how you come down." So it will be wise to know the basic mechanics of jumping.

1. Speed of travel. Your takeoff speed influences the distance you cover in the jump and the height you attain. At first, practice at very slow skating speeds, working up gradually to faster speeds. Take notice of the different distances you cover between takeoff and landing.

2. Height. Remember that jumping means rising *up*—not thrusting forward. Your body angle at takeoff should be erect so that you land on your skate. Whether you are doing an edge or toe-assisted takeoff, your job is to rise straight in the air off the correct edge. Don't worry about distance—good old gravity and your speed will handle that department.

Flight. All revolution jumps may be performed with either clockwise or counterclockwise rotation. You'll probably find at the outset, however, that you are either a "right-handed" or "left-handed" skater; that is, more comfortable with one rotation direction than the other. Don't let this bother you—in competition, judges do not hold one direction more sacred than the other as long as good form is achieved. The skater who can rotate *both* ways, however, is the consummate jumping virtuoso. (Tommy Andrew relates the story of Natalie Dunn, our national and world freestyle champion, who was a confirmed lefthanded skater early in her career. Learning to jump and spin in both directions took many extra hours of patience and fortitude.)

Form. Body control is the major factor in your overall form. We have only discussed three air positions (standard, split, and stag), but learning other "novelty" positions will round out your skating performances: *Mazurka*—legs downward, feet crossed at the knee; *Russian split*—straddle position, with arms extended in the same direction as the legs; *Arch Back*—back bend in the air, arms and legs also curved back; *Tuck position*—skates under the body almost in sitting position.

Jumping Hints

• *Your landing should be as graceful and effortless as your takeoff.*

• *While in the air, your landing foot is the "action" foot. It should be raised slightly higher and set down before the free skate.*

• *Press the shoulders in the opposite direction of the jump to correct for over-rotation and slipping when you land. If this is a problem, practicing three-turns and school figures should help you considerably with shoulder rotation.*

• *At landing, your free leg acts as a rudder, so its control is vital in steering you onto your next edge and direction. Don't let it drop to the floor before your landing skate or waggle to one side or the other.*

SPINS

A *spin* is defined as at least three continuous rotations around a stationary axis. The stationary axis is an imaginary line that passes up from your spotted skate(s) *through* your body; that is, three loops (see chapter 9 on figure skating) would not technically comprise a spin because the stationary axis of the circle created does not pass through the body. Thus, the tracing made by your skate during the revolutions—were it visible—would ideally be a solid ring, rather than a moving "chain" of rings.

As with jumps, spins may be classified as either two-foot or one-foot spins.

Two-Foot Spins

You should begin with a simple two-foot spin, picturing yourself as a drill boring a hole into the floor.

a. Applying pressure to the inside of your left skate, wind up your shoulders to the right.

b. Unwind shoulders, spinning to the left (counterclockwise) rotating on the RIF-LIB edge. Practice until you can complete three revolutions in good form.

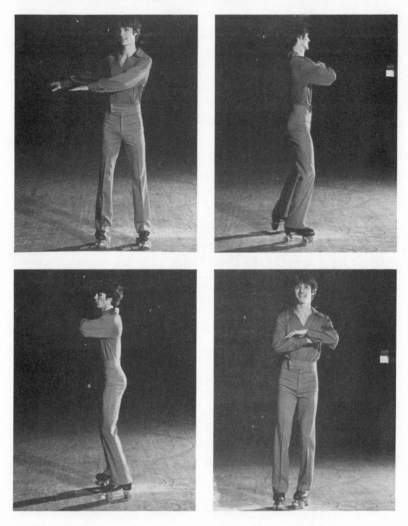

Two-Foot Spin

One-Foot Spins

One-foot spins may further be broken down into three categories:

1. Upright—the body remains erect.

2. Sit—the hipline is as low or lower than the skating knee. The free leg is sometimes extended parallel to the floor as in the shoot-the-duck position.

Upright Spin

Sit Spins

3. Camel—the body from head to free foot is parallel to the floor.

To begin a one-foot spin, first do a two-foot spin for one revolution and then lift your right foot about six inches. Transfer all your weight onto the front of your left skate, revolving on an LIB edge. (To spin to the right, reverse the directions.)

With two feet, eight wheels, and two toe stops, these jumps and spins are obviously just a sampling of what is possible. Add

Camel Spins

to these the various positions you can create with your arms, head, and free leg, whether balletic or modern, the different speeds of the spins, (that you can change *during* the spins), and the combinations you can perform with jump-spins, and you can see why freestyle is the most exciting aspect of roller skating.

FOOTWORK

As mentioned earlier in this chapter, your footwork—the skating that links together the jumps and spins—is as important to your overall routine as the jumps and spins themselves. To quote again from the RSROA's *Free Skating Manual,*

> Link steps between the spins and jumps should be arranged so that each movement blends into the next, in harmony with the program's selection of music. Laying out the Free Skating program onto the skating surface should be well planned and not left to chance during the actual performance. Footwork will set the basic pattern or design of the program and the jumps and spins will then be executed in various and advantageous spots on the skating surface.

Thus, if you are thinking of preparing a full skating routine make sure you include a full helping of turns (Mohawk, threes, etcetera) and link steps. Use all parts of the skating surface and choose music that will give you the best presentation for your skating skills.

PAIRS FREESTYLE

Pairs freestyle reaches for the pinnacle of the sport; pairs performances combine all skating skills into a coherent artistic composition that must be synchronized not only to music but to the partner's movements as well. Good pairs teams seem to skate with the spontaneous ease of a single skater, as if the two partners had merged physically and spiritually.

The routines must exhibit skill in two areas, and in fact the teams receive two scores from the judges: content and manner (style).

Pairs Freestyle Movements

Program Content: Variety and Difficulty

As in individual freestyle skating competition, pair members must show versatility over the entire range of spins, jumps, and footwork, both in contact with one another and individually. The added element in pairs is the lifts. Over the past few years there has been a great deal of emphasis placed on lifts, and possibly because of this, pairs freestyle has been experiencing a slight decline in the number of pairs teams that do well in competition. Finding boys big and strong enough to accomplish the lifts (especially at the younger levels) is proving difficult. However, there is talk in some circles of a "return to skating" movement—emphasizing individual and contact spins and footwork and devaluating the more athletic (though breathtaking) lifts.

Lifts, spins, and jumps are all classified according to difficulty, and the judges will examine this aspect of performance very carefully in determining the team's variety score. Thus, the team should be certain its program includes movements that rise to the Class A and B level. (See the USAC *Roller Freeskating Manual* for the classification of jumps, spins, and lifts.)

Manner of Performance

The second part of a pair's team score, "manner of performance," is judged according to five characteristics: harmony of movement, form, virtuosity, interpretation, and arrangement. Harmony refers to such elements as harmonious execution of lifts, position in contact spins, and taking off and landing simultaneously on jumps. Form entails the skaters' overall style in spinning, jumping, and skating. Virtuosity covers the qualitative aspects of your movements: speed and spotting of spins, height of jumps, sureness of landings, etc. Interpretation and arrangement cover the thematic and musical components of your program: the way you translate the rhythm and mood of the music into the physical movement, the continuity of your program, use of the entire skating surface, and so forth.

11

The Racer's Edge: Speed Skating

Every year, thousands of young skaters—both boys and girls —race around a 100-meter oval track in head-to-head speed skating competitions. Speed skating has a unique appeal for young children; the race against the clock and against other kids of the same age and sex captures an excitement unparalleled by the more staid and individualistic branches of artistic skating.

There are fourteen different "classes" of races in USAC sanctioned competitions, each class delineated according to age, sex, and race distance. For example, boys 8 to 10 years old race against other boys of the same age over distances of 200, 300, and 400 meters (2, 3, and 4 times around the track, respectively); the class of "freshman girls" (12 to 14 years old) race 300, 500, and 1,000 meters against girls of the same age. As the ages of the competitors increase so does the range of distances they must race. And, besides the individual races, there are two- and four-member relay races in which the competitors must participate as well.

Training of a Speed Skater

If you want to become a competitive speed skater, you must be willing to undergo a rigorous training program. Depending on your coach, practice sessions can go anywhere from one to

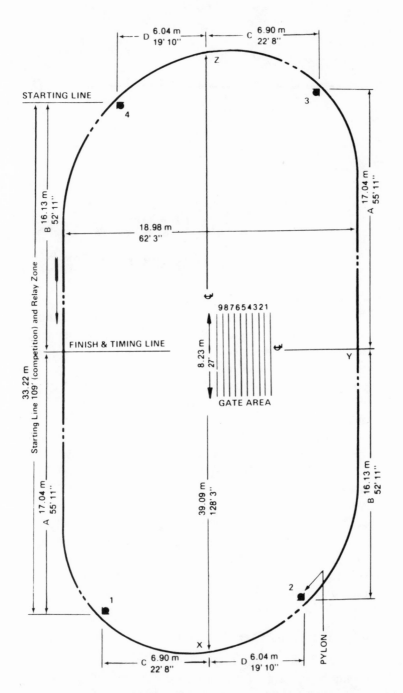

Official Championship 100 Meter Track (USAC)

"If no one's looking . . . . " (RSROA).

two hours each, three to five times each week, which means hundreds upon hundreds of laps as you near meet time. At Sacramento's Holiday Skating Plaza, Ron Jerue, coach of Kenny Hutton (first American to win a medal in World competition), runs his skaters through three practice sessions each week. "Two sessions was just not enough," he explains. "The time lapses in between caused too much muscle tightening."

Grady Merrell of the Skate Ranch in Santa Ana (which has qualified more skaters for world competition than any other rink) uses a five-practice-session-per-week schedule. Both coaches believe in the benefits of specialized training, such as bicycle riding and running, because of the similarity in leg-muscle exertion. Merrell has special praise for uphill running—a great endurance-builder. Jerue's older skaters sometimes lift weights for upper body development, perhaps a new area of speed skating training; his younger skaters start with calisthenics (pushups, situps) and jumping rope for calf muscle strengthening and overall agility.

Girls love racing too (RSROA).

The structure of the meets dictates that skaters must have the stamina to go fifty laps—and still have enough speed left over to sprint in the relays. In this sense the speed skater must be much more versatile than the track runner, who usually specializes in either sprints, middle-distances, or long-distances.

A common training program for a beginning speed skater would be something like the following:

1. Practice in stepping sideways.

2. Skating circles (forward crosspulls).

3. Skating on the track—where to coast, using the least amount of steps, using "push" power rather than "run" power.

4. Two-lap races. ("The slower skaters can't get too far behind in these shorter races," Jerue points out, "and so they don't get discouraged or lose interest too quickly.")

5. Longer races—where to be in relation to the wall and pylons, where and how to take a corner, and so forth.

Diet for Speed

Eating right is also very important for the beginning speed skater, especially for the fourteen-to-eighteen-year-old rapid growth age bracket. Vitamin-supplemented diets are sometimes recommended, and at least one top coach encourages liver pills for stamina-building.

Coaches seem to be evenly divided on the advisability of carbohydrate-loading, a practice used by long-distance runners, whereby the competitor eats food high in carbohydrates the few days prior to a race.

Strategies and Psychology

As in all physical endeavors, the mind plays an important role in skating performance on the speed track. Tremendous speeds are attained by speed skaters (upwards of 35 mph), so the fear element is a vital one to overcome. "Psychologically speaking, the coach's job is to gear his coaching skills to each skater on a *specific* basis," Grady Merrell advocates. "Each skater is different and needs different kinds of encouragement. The main thing to understand is that training is a *year 'round* proposition. It's too late to start psyching up your team at the last minute."

Ken Sutton, Junior Men's Speed Champion (RSROA)

Similar sentiments from Ron Jerue:

"A year of good, solid practice makes for a confident frame of mind when that big meet rolls around."

Race strategy, of course, is almost as important as speed; valuable seconds and meters can be gained if the skater knows when to and when not to pass another skater. He or she should be alert to the "patterns" of every other skater in a particular race. For example, a skater who coasts during one stretch of the track, and then coasts again, can be a good bet to do it a third time—this is the time for the off-the-pace skater to step on the gas and pass.

Quick passes into the track (left side of lead skater) can be utilized much more easily now than just a few years ago thanks to the softer speed wheels, which have greater gripping power. Learning starting-line technique, especially for the shorter sprints, becomes an enormous advantage.

The speed skater should be aware not to get caught in a "box"—two or more skaters intentionally or unintentionally preventing another from passing. Various illegal strategies are fouls and may lead to disqualification by the referee:

Blocking. Preventing another skater from passing by an unnatural method—with or without body contact.

Charging. A passing skater causing contact with the overtaken skater that disrupts the overtaken skater's natural progress.

Elbowing. The deliberate use of elbows that interferes with another skater's progress.

Jamming. Suddenly slowing up, causing the skaters behind you to run into each other.

Riding in (or out). Swerving into another skater's line of travel.

Further information on all aspects of speed skating may be gotten from the United States Amateur Confederation of Roller Skating, 7700 "A" Street, Lincoln, Nebraska 68510.

12

The World of Competition and Showmanship

Ask your typical American 100 percent dyed-in-the-wool rabid sports fan who the national or world roller skating champions are and you will most likely receive a look as blank as the television he has just turned off. Very few people—very few skaters for that matter—know that there *are* champions; over the years roller skating competitions have gotten about as much publicity as domino tournaments.

Well there are champions, have been for forty years in some branches of skating, and the national and world women's free-style champion for the past three years is one in the same person, Natalie Dunn of Bakersfield, California. She is twenty-two years old and the first woman ever to do a triple jump in competition.

TRAINING FOR THE TOP

Beginning skaters with visions of someday entering competition would be wise to know ahead of time the investment of time required. Ron Jellse of Harp's Rollerdrome in Cincinnati, a man who has coached more champions than anyone, holds practice sessions for his advanced skaters every day. The sessions run three-and-one-half hours (usually 3:30 to 7:00 after

Kimberly Campbell, International Singles Champion (RSROA)

school). During vacations and right before big meets, practice time sometimes goes as long as eight hours a day.

But the beginning skater needn't worry about training schedules just yet. For quite a few months he or she should adhere to something like the following program before entering competitions.

1. *Basic lessons.* Practice the exercises given in chapters 3 to 7 and take basic instruction at your local rink.

2. *Learn American style dance skating.* At least enough to qualify for the top level of Bronze Proficiency Tests.

3. *Learn basic figures.* This might require patience and fortitude, but most coaches highly recommend it for the rewards it will later bring to freestyle.

4. *Take RSROA proficiency tests in dance and figures.* You will not be competing against anyone else, but the tests will give you experience performing in pressure situations.

5. *Begin freestyle practice.* At least one-half hour per day—every day if possible. Do exercises, such as the ones outlined in chapter 16, to increase the flexibility and strength of the skating muscles.

6. *Enter local competitions.* Before thinking about regional and national meets, enter small competitions in your home town. Try competitions in all branches of skating to see which you are best in. (Contact your local RSROA-affiliated rink for information.)

SPECIALIZED TRAINING

When you become serious about becoming a competitive skater, specialized training in two areas will give you a big edge (so to speak) over the other skaters: dance and weight training.

Ballet Instruction

Lessons from an experienced ballet teacher can provide you with important training that your skating teacher might have little experience in. "A definite necessity for the competition freestyle or dance skater," says Ron Jellse. The following are just some of the areas with which ballet can help you:

• *Posture.* Helps to form a straight back, good turnout of the free leg, graceful movement.

• *Choreography.* Especially in the area of music interpretation and footwork.

• *Strength and flexibility.* Rail or "bar exercises" develop both qualities, especially for the arms, an often neglected but nevertheless important part of the skater's body.

• *Expression.* This will be part of your score in any dance or freestyle competition. With good, interpretive expression, you can turn a judge's head your way.

• *Breathing.* Ballet will teach you proper breathing techniques that will stand you in good stead during the more difficult parts of your program. Proper breathing is also necessary to develop stamina.

Bar Exercises for Skaters

Weight Training

In this time of heavy emphasis on lifts in pairs freestyle skating, the male partner of the team must be strong enough to lift the female gracefully and with ease. For younger boys the best place to start is with pushups, which will develop the biceps and triceps muscles of the arms necessary to accomplish the primary lifts (most notably the "extension lift"). As time goes on, the boy should think about the possibility of a weight training program to increase strength of the upper body.

PSYCHOLOGY: THE COACH'S JOB

The methods a coach utilizes during practices and right before competitions vary from skater to skater. Each skater is different, and the coach should know each well enough to handle personalities, strengths, weaknesses, and idiosyncracies on an individualized basis. For example, some skaters' performances are hurt very badly after watching other skaters perform; in other cases, watching improves performance.

Linda Todd and Charles Kirshner, 1977 International Junior Dance Champions (RSROA)

Approaching the big moment of the meet, most successful coaches emphasize performance rather than give pep talks. Accenting the skater's strengths reinforces the skater's confidence in his or her own ability. "Tell them aobut their mistakes right before a contest and that's what they'll do," Ron Jellse explains.

The ability to do well in competition does not come from last-minute instruction. "The skater should be prepared for the competition *before* the competition," Tommy Andrew affirms. "New teachers often go into a frenzy when a skater makes an error in the warm-up, and it's a mistake. There is too much going on for a skater to be expected to retain the instruction. In fact, often the opposite happens—the skater becomes fixated on the movement and winds up missing it during performance."

Skaters will pick up the coach's attitudes, so the coach must be careful to control emotions and project confidence. There are some excellent teachers who are lousy at competitions. Teachers of champions have an inner sense about what to do and not to do at competitions, a charisma like that of their champion skaters that brings out the best in performance.

THE GOLD SKATE CLASSIC

On entering one of the older rinks that have somehow managed to survive the American Disco Deluge and Strobe Light City, you have the sensation of going back in time. After spending a day in the real world, it's hard to believe people are still doing things like "The Glide Waltz" and "The Academy Blues" in gymnasiumlike rollerdomes.

If some of these rather refreshing anachronisms seem like 1930s soup kitchens, the Gold Skate Classic, an annual skating extravaganza put on annually in Bakersfield, California, is something like an 1890s ice cream parlor. Thousands of skaters of all shapes, sizes, and ages, dressed as panda bears, rag dolls, black-face minstrels, Mother-Goose characters, Mexican flamenco dancers, and HMS Pinafore sailors, parade their wares, hopping and skipping around the stage floor in elaborate mini and maxi "production numbers." They come from all over California for this one—it is *the* skaters weekend.

To the nonskating observer Gold Skate looks something like

Gold Skate Classic

a Busby Berkeley musical on wheels, that is, if there *were* any nonskaters. The only ones to qualify for this title, however, are the hot dog vendors, a few local media people, and the six hundred hacks writing roller skating books. The Gold Skate Classic, produced every year by Joe Nazarro and G. B. "Budd" Van Roekel, is above all a show put on by skaters, performed by skaters, for an audience of skaters.

Every February, the rinks send their representatives to wonderful, dust-ridden, downtown Bakersfield where every Holiday Inn, Travelodge, and Motel 6 within a ten-mile radius has been booked solid for months. Though Bakersfield is a relatively big skating town (home of World Champion Natalie Dunn), the townspeople couldn't care less about Gold Skate, except, of course, for the revenue the show brings into Howard Johnson's, Denny's, and Jack-in-the-Box.

But the skaters care. For the most part these are not your typical recreational skaters (the "new breed"), but the old-timers, the skaters who remember the days of wooden wheels and skate keys.

And the kids love it. For most of them it is the big moment of their young lives, a chance to perform before real spotlights and three thousand people.

Throughout two solid days of skating, singles, pairs, artistic dance teams, groups, and production numbers strut their stuff in, around, and through Bakersfield Civic Center. And these are not bum-skaters. Generally speaking, indoor competitive skaters are head and wheels over even the most polished outdoor skaters. Many of the skaters who show up at the Gold Skate are the best competitive skaters in California, who find the Gold Skate a perfect opportunity to train for and preview routines they will use to win regional and national championships.

Gold Skate Classic

Roller Hockey in the parks.

ROLLER HOCKEY—THE TEAM SKATING SPORT

Except for the speed skating relay races, the only team skating sport is roller hockey. So if team sports interest you more than individual sports, roller hockey is for you.

With its roots in the New York streets (as early as 1922, the New York Parks Dept. organized playground teams into tournaments held in Central Park), roller hockey is now organized in more than fifty countries, with large participation in Spain and Portugal.

PART 4

STRICTLY OUTDOORS

13

Wings on Your Heels

The outdoor skating surge owes as much to the physical fitness phenomenon of the 1970s as it does to traditional rink skating of the last hundred years. For the most part, the recreational skaters who fill the country's parks, boardwalks, and streets every weekend do not fill the rinks on weekdays. There is overlap (especially park to roller disco) and there will probably be much more carryover as skating becomes more popular, but for now the outdoor whizzer digs zooming around in the fresh air and sunshine, loves flying through the trees or by the ocean —in short, loves outdoor skating for the *outdoors* as much as for the skating.

Though you might get some argument from New York's Central Park skaters, the outdoor craze seems to have started in California, which is no surprise considering the congenial weather, space, and smooth seaside skating surfaces. Very early Saturday and Sunday mornings, people line up at Skates on Haight in San Francisco, Cheapskates on the Venice boardwalk, Good Skates in New York, or one of the many portable van operations that flock to the skating areas on weekends, some diehard enthusiasts enduring waits of two or three hours.

"Americans love wheels," says Lee Cole, young entrepreneur-owner of Skates on Haight. When the skateboarding craze began to die out a few years ago, Lee converted his skateboard shop to a skating "clearing house" of equipment, skating

125

Skating by the sea in Santa Monica.

shows, and other skating events in the Bay Area. "First bicycles, then the automobile, and now skates. But riding a bike can be tough work at times; you can compare it to a car with manual transmission. Skating is speed and power—automatic transmission."

Over the past two years, business has tripled at Skates on Haight, and no doubt many more skating stores are forthcoming. Skates occupy almost no storage space, have no electrical parts or complex mechanical gears, so they rarely need repair.

"When they do need repair," says Cole, "I can take care of them in five minutes. We're a busy, on-the-go people. Repairs while-you-wait is a distinct advantage."

Some skating stores are becoming distributors for the skate manufacturers; one of them is Jeff Rosenberg's "Cheapskates" operation on the Venice boardwalk, the first outdoor skating outlet. "It's an ego trip of mine," he is quoted by *Roller Skating* magazine. "I believe that I was the first one to do it, and it is now growing into an international phenomenon."

Unlike tennis or golf, skating has no real aristocratic heritage. Skating is a working class sport—cheap, fun, a way to blow off steam and stay in shape. Strangely enough, outdoor skating might be something of a rebellion against one part of the fitness craze:

"Those joggers were driving me nuts," says one park skater. "Huffing and puffing like buffaloes. They say they're having a great time, but to me they look like wounded animals in heat."

Skates on Haight—Buy or rent for time well spent.

Skating Your Dog

Another Golden Gate Park skater expressed similar sentiments. "The jogging situation in the park was getting so bad, it was worse than when they allowed cars through here. You couldn't walk around without getting run over by a bunch of joggers."

(Now, of course, you can hardly walk around the park without getting run over by a bunch of skaters.)

SKATING AND "THE SCENE"

Whether skating is a better form of exercise than running (or any other sport, for that matter) will no doubt become a hotly debated issue in the next few years among those interested in major problems of contemporary society. However, the sport of roller skating does seem inextricably bound with the need of twentieth-century humankind to transcend its physical and material limitations. While Asian cultures have historically used internal techniques (yoga, meditation, etc.) and these methods have taken root to some extent in the west, western civilization has been much more enamored of technology for relieving the burdens of the body and the outside world. Like hang-gliding, skydiving, race car driving, and skiing, lacing up a pair of skates is an attempt—however primitive—to put wings on our heels; skates are our twentieth-century anti-gravity boots.

Learning is Half the Fun.

Mr. Tommy Tunes—for your listening pleasure.

While rink skating revolves (and revolves) around the artistic
and detailed aspects of dance, freestyle, and figures, the additional space granted by the great outdoors encourages dare-
devilry, tricks, and speed. In Venice, two of the great crowd-
attracters are the trash-can jumping and beer-can slalom
events. In San Francisco, skaters such as Tommy Tunes, who
plays the accordion on skates, and the Karamazov Brothers,
who juggle on skates, have become definite skating personali-

"Barrel" jumping in Venice.

ties. Terry Caccia of Venice, the recognized innovator of "wind-skating," zooms with a sail that catches the ocean winds and sends him up to speeds of thirty-five miles per hour.

Outdoor skating also has its functional purposes. The gliding movements and leg muscles used in skating are very similar to those used in skiing—and a good way for skiers to keep in shape in the off-season.

SKATING—TRANSPORTATION FOR THE EIGHTIES?

The idea of roller skating becoming a major mode of transportation in the 1980s is not as farfetched as it might sound. After all, something will have to be done to reduce the stranglehold of the automobile, and the inefficiency, noise, congestion, and air pollution that mass reliance on the automobile creates, not to mention the inadequacy of mass transportation—dirty, crowded subways, late buses, expensive taxis.

Skaters can easily attain speeds of fifteen to twenty miles per hour on flat surfaces; simple arithmetic shows that a twenty-mile commute that takes an hour by car on the Hollywood Freeway during rush hour can be done just as quickly by a good skater—given, of course, the proper road conditions. Workers who are interested in staying fit, but who don't have the time for exercising, might put two and two together and lead city planners to try experimenting with "skating lanes" as they have with bicycle lanes in some smaller communities.

Rolling Tongue-in-Chic

As far as the future is concerned, the potentialities for skating are enormous:

• Think how quickly your postman could deliver the mail on skates. Or your paperboy finish his route. Or your utility man read your gas and electric meters.

• How about the guys who sweep up after the fans leave the stadium, auditorium, or concert hall?

• Imagine how much easier (and how much more fun) the office boy's job of delivering memos would be if he could skate from office to office rather than walk.

• Attention housewives! Skate through the aisles of your supermarket; you'll take off as many calories as you put into your basket and still have time for your favorite afternoon soaps.

• Politicians: Worry no longer about walking tours through rough neighborhoods. Skate through them in half the time.

• And doctors will have no more excuses about missing emergency calls in hospitals with skates zipping them from ward to ward.

Skating my baby back home.

Yes, this is only banter—for the time being, anyway. How far any fad will go in America usually depends on how far the corporate structure is willing to exploit it. Remember that the automobile, steamboat, and airplane all began as novelties, mere follies, until the controllers of production recognized their potential for efficiency which, translated, means their capacity for increasing profits.

As a means of transportation, roller skating has certainly reached the status of "novelty." A handful of "eccentrics" skate to work, and on many college campuses students roll from class to class. As managers, bureaucrats, and city planners discover the money-saving element in skating you can expect to see more skating for fun and profit.

You can also expect to see more ultra-modern skating centers and roller discos (such as the one opened by Good Skates owner Judy Lynn in mid-town New York and Cher's rink in Hollywood), roller skating marathons (the first already planned for Long Beach in spring 1979). The Greenpeace Skatathon in San Francisco's Golden Gate Park raised $75,000, including $5,000 from rock star Graham Nash and his skating team, "The Non-Aerosol Rollons."

Riding the walls (Bob Kingsbook photo)

"Radical Skating"

A term used for any outdoor skating done on a nonflat surface, *radical skating* is pretty hot stuff among the teenagers on the west coast, so you easterners can expect to see "skateparks" very soon. Once the private domain of skateboarders, these concrete undulating bowl-mazes look something like what would happen if Salvador Dali were allowed to design our sidewalks. Now the roller-coaster-like chutes and steep bowls are filled with roller skaters, who have discovered that incredible stunts can be performed even better *wearing* wheels than riding them.

Hitching a ride...

. . . Sometimes pays off.

A well-earned rest after a hard day's skate.

Safety Hints for Outdoor Skating

- *If you're going to zoom, don't zoom out of blind alleys or around blind corners.*

- *As best as you are able in pothole-riddled America, stay away from broken, rough, or sandy surfaces—and watch out for objects on the road (rocks, toys, glass).*

- *Don't skate in the street unless it is specifically marked for skating use, that is, unless cars are prohibited.*

- *Hitching onto buses, bikes and other vehicles is a no-no (hitching onto another skater is okay).*

- *Always check your equipment before skating. Make certain you have no loose nuts or bolts.*

- *Before crossing street intersections watch for motorized monsters.*

- *Show courtesy to those nonrolling creatures, pedestrians. Who knows? You too may find yourself walking sometime and you don't want to develop bad karma.*

- *Avoid hills. If you do skate down a hill, make sure you have enough room to slalom or traverse the hill. If you realize you can't stop, don't ride out the hill praying for an angel to save you at the bottom; skate over to the side, to a building or parking meter, and hold on.*

- *Lastly, don't skate in the rain. Urethane, your wheel substance, loses its traction in water. Bearings are moving parts; they will rust in the rain.*

14

Roller Games for Children 5-50

Though it is a bit difficult to imagine dribbling a basketball or pole vaulting on roller skates, virtually any game or sport that can be played on feet can be played on skates. The most popular outdoor skating games, roller-frisbee, roller football, and roller hockey, are very difficult to adapt to indoor areas. However, games like limbo, shuttle skate, and slalom skating, which require less space, are equally as effective indoors as out.

Limbo

All that's needed for this game in the way of equipment is:

• Two poles about four feet high, with pegs spaced at six-inch intervals for adjusting the height of the crossbar.

• One crossbar (a broomstick would do).

The object of the game is to skate under the bar without knocking it off its perch. The skater who can go the lowest is the winner. (As you really get down, you'll have to go under in shoot-the-duck position.)

If you have enough room, a good variation of the game is using three limbo set-ups arranged in a straight or slalom pattern and with different crossbar heights, forming a limbo course in which a timer can be used for added dimension.

Besides being a lot of fun, the game develops balance and body control.

Backward through the slalom course.

Slalom

Equipment:

• Six to twelve rubber pylons (actually any set of uniform objects will work, such as milk cartons or soda cans).

To start, place the pylons at ten-foot intervals along a straightaway: the object is to zigzag through the pylons without knocking any over. As time goes on, decrease the space between pylons, which creates a more difficult course.

Variations include (1) arranging the course on a downhill slope, and (2) skating in different body positions (camel, shoot-the-duck). Using a timer makes for more excitement because the skaters who go closest to the pylons will get the best times.

The game teaches body lean and edge control.

Roller Frisbee

Frisbee has been one of the most popular games in America in recent years and the sport adapts easily to roller skates. Skating adds extra dimension to the many trick Frisbee throws and catches (read *Frisbee by the Masters* by Charles Tips, Celestial Arts: Millbrae, California), and the many Frisbee games—ultimate Frisbee, Frisbee football—also lend themselves easily to skating speed and action.

Around the University of California (Berkeley) and New York's Central Park, where Frisbee golf courses have been mapped out for years, golfers have recently taken to wearing skates to roll from hole to hole rather than walk.

Roller Frisbee.

Roller Hockey

Roller Football

The game can be played in any playground or schoolyard. It is played just like touch football, except that the participants are advised to wear protective equipment—pads and helmets—because falling is inevitable.

Shuttle

Equipment:

- Two buckets or pails
- Twelve wooden or plastic blocks

This is a racing game in which two teams may be pitted against one another as in a relay race. The skaters race to a pile of blocks, pick one up without stopping, and skate to a bucket where the block is deposited. The first team to finish is the winner.

Shuttle improves edge control and speed.

PART 5

FOR THE
HEALTH OF IT

15

Rollercizing for Weight Control and Fitness

Allen Selner, M. D.

This chapter and chapter 16 were researched and written by Dr. Allen Selner in conjunction with the authors. Dr. Selner, a podiatrist practicing in Sherman Oaks, California, specializes in sports medicine. He is currently Co-Chairman of the Department of Sports Medicine, Southern California Podiatric Medical Center, and a clinical researcher on the biomechanics of roller skating at UCLA.

For normal physical and mental development, exercise is essential. Exercise increases the efficiency of the heart, decreases body weight and body fat content, and tones and shapes the muscles of the body. To accomplish these goals, specific exercises are designed for specific purposes and problems. However, there are basic rules to follow when deciding on any exercise program.

Recently, it has been discovered that maximum benefits can only be obtained through repetitive and prolonged exercise. This means that any exercise program must be done a minimum of three to four times each week for thirty to forty minutes each exercise period. If the program is not maintained at these minimal levels, the benefits of exercise are not nearly as great. Therefore, such sports as golf or bowling are not nearly as effective for good cardiovascular and musculoskeletal exercise. They certainly have their place as recreational sports, but are not effective for good aerobic training.

You can sail on land . . .

The need for continuous, repetitive exercise is based on the body's reaction to stress. To strengthen the heart and lung efficiencies, stress must be applied to the body. Less strenuous sports may burn only 100 to 200 calories per hour, whereas *roller skating will burn approximately 360 calories per hour*—a very significant difference.

Aerobic Exercise

Each individual responds differently to stress. The way this is monitored is through the pulse rate. The ideal pulse rate for an individual with a normal heart and body is found to be roughly 70 percent of the quantity 220, minus the individual's age. This pulse rate should be maintained during exercise to gain the maximum benefits available. At this pulse rate, an individual experiences what is called the *aerobic level*, which means using all available oxygen to fuel the energy system of the body.

Or sail hand-in-hand.

Going beyond this point, an athlete is unable to breathe the needed amount of oxygen and goes into "oxygen debt." The body, unable to get sufficient oxygen, prompts biochemical changes resulting in a build-up of lactic acid. This chemical causes muscles to become tired and sore, forcing the individual to slow down. This is why speed skating (and other stressful exercises) results in muscle fatigue.

Trimming Body Fat

At the aerobic level, the body is burning mostly fat as an energy source. Thus, it is ideal for trimming excessive body fat. It is important to differentiate at this time between body weight and body fat.

People often say: "I weigh the same as I did when I was in high school." This is a very misleading statement, for it implies

---

Skating for Fitness

• Children with coordination difficulties such as cerebral palsy will find skating to be extremely beneficial for developing improved muscular tone and coordination. Children who have had difficulty participating in other sports will find skating an enjoyable outlet for their athletic endeavors.

• People who have had heart attacks and who are on cardiac rehabilitation programs will find that skating supplies just the right amount of exercise to help them back on a good road to recovery. (However, the heart attack patient should consult his or her doctor before skating.)

• Wear knee or elbow pads if you are having problems with abrasions on either of these areas. Wrist guards are also available for those who fall very frequently. Be safety conscious to prevent injuries.

• Any clothing that is restrictive will make turning difficult. This is especially important when you are falling because if you are unable to move properly, you cannot go with the fall and will often become more seriously injured. Wear loose fitting clothing.

that an individual is as healthy and in as good shape as he or she was in high school. Unfortunately, while body weight may remain the same, more than likely the amount of body fat has increased and the amount of muscle tissue has decreased. Therefore, even though body weight is maintained, there is excessive fat and too little muscle.

This is detrimental to a weight reduction program in that muscle will burn calories, but fat tissue will not. The ideal man should be roughly 15 percent body fat and the woman roughly 22 percent body fat. Diet alone will not keep an individual balanced at this point. Exercise is a critical factor in maintaining an ideal lean body mass and low body-fat content.

When comparing various exercises, we must examine factors such as aerobic level to determine which exercises are most beneficial. Running, for example, supplies very good aerobic

---

• If you are having problems fitting boots, remember that the better boots come in half sizes instead of full sizes. They also come in variable widths, and custom boots are available through major companies. Rather than suffer with ill-fitting boots, shop for good quality boots so that fitting will be less of a problem.

• Leather boots are better than synthetic vinyl boots. Synthetic materials tend to keep moisture in the boot. Also, leather tends to mold around the foot better than vinyls.

• When fitting skates for children, parents often buy skates two sizes too large to allow the child to grow into them. This sounds logical theoretically, but often the practice causes ill-fitting loose boots with greater chances of injury to the child.

• If you feel a great deal of lower leg and ankle fatigue, the truck assembly on the bottom of the skate might be too tight. These wheel attachments can be adjusted according to your weight and skating ability. If you are working too hard while turning, these trucks can be loosened by rink or skating shop personnel.

training if done consistently several times per week. The negative aspects of running are that injuries are frequent and many people do not enjoy it enough to maintain the exercise over a long period of time.

For exercise to be beneficial it must be done regularly and be enjoyable enough to maintain over a long period of time. Skating meets both of these criteria. It is continuous, moderately stressful exercise and thus increases the pulse rate. Because there is very little trauma, injuries are few. Most importantly, it is very, very enjoyable, and the compliance rate is very high. Individuals who have not been on an exercise program will find that this sport is ideal in that they do not require a lot of stress to raise their pulse rate to the ideal level.

In the past, roller skating has been looked upon as mere recreation. Nothing could be further from the truth. Skating and the flexibility and strength skating exercises (outlined in the next chapter) will provide you with a fun, efficient way to develop good health and fitness. Moreover, skating is a great muscle-toning exercise. Individuals with heavy thighs and legs can slim and tone by skating regularly.

16

Skating Biomechanics, Exercises, and Injury Prevention
Allen Selner, M. D.

The average skater does not usually concentrate on the coordination of arm, foot, and leg movement. He merely attempts to move forward in a nice, easy, slow manner. However, to perform even simple forward locomotion, a great many activities must be integrated. Individuals with flat or high-arched feet, bowlegs, pigeon-toed stances, knock-knees, and a variety of other structural variations will perform these maneuvers differently, and with varying degrees of success.

Let's examine the exact mechanics of forward skating. First, and most importantly, it must be understood that forward edges and turns are skated by applying pressure to the wheels. It is therefore essential to understand the leg-muscle-foot-skate-surface linkage because anything interfering with this linkage will result in problems for the skater. The analogy to an automobile flat tire is appropriate here. Not only is the flat tire a problem, but because of the unevenness of the wheels, steering becomes extremely difficult.

IMPORTANCE OF WELL-FITTING BOOTS

No matter how tightly the skating boot fits around the foot, foot motion inside the boot is inevitable. However, excessive play in the boot causes great difficulty in transmitting the necessary force to the inside wheels to accomplish inside edges and turns and jumps that take off from inside edges.

153

Many times, individuals with flat or pronated feet have the same difficulty, and are also susceptible to inside knee pain. Again, this is a linkage factor. As the foot flattens out, the leg turns in. These two events cannot be separated. The same individuals may develop shin splints, knee pain, and hip pain while running. Fortunately, these problems can be prevented by placing devices that restrict foot motions within the boot.

The problem may be compounded because muscles will try to prevent motions resulting in fatigue or pain in the leg, thigh, or low back, causing the body to go out of alignment. It is very much like having a visual problem. If you are nearsighted or farsighted and straining your eyes trying to read, very commonly headaches will occur. It is much the same way with skating. If the lower extremity is malaligned, secondary problems can result.

Fortunately, because skating does not require slapping the foot against the ground, these problems are far, far less serious as compared with running. However, the mechanics of alignment are critical in turning properly and skating with ease. One cannot force the body to perform. It must be tuned and aligned properly for maximum efficiency.

FLEXIBILITY EXERCISES

Before participating in any active sport, it is essential to warm up. This is important for several reasons. Muscle tissue is the only tissue that can be significantly stretched and contracted. Muscles are attached to tendons, which are attached to bones. When muscles contract, the fibers interlock. This contraction shortens the muscle, thus pulling on the tendon, which pulls on the bone. This is the way motion is carried out.

Muscles are very complex parts of the body and require adequate care to perform well. Before exercising, the muscles need to be warmed; the actual physical temperature must be increased to prepare the muscle for action that follows. To do this properly and effectively, warmup exercises must be done slowly and with no bouncing. The stretches should be held for approximately ten to fifteen seconds, and then released. Exercises, such as jumping jacks and touching the toes, are entirely inadequate to achieve these purposes. Indeed, as one bounces to touch one's toes, a muscle reflex fires, resulting in a contraction rather than a stretch.

To avoid reflex contractions, stretching should be done while the muscle is relaxed and the body is in a good position. Also, you should stretch all muscles that require it. Certain muscles, especially the ones in the back of the legs, tend to be shorter and stronger than the ones in the front of the legs. Because of these imbalances in strength and flexibility, it is essential to stretch each muscle individually to warm them and allow for increased flexibility. It is no fun to begin skating only to pull a muscle because of an abrupt maneuver. This is very unfortunate, especially if it could have been avoided.

Calf Stretch

The calf muscle attaches behind the knee and goes down through the back of the leg attaching to the heel bone. It is the muscle used to push off in forward skating, so it is essential for this muscle to be strong and flexible. To stretch this muscle, stand against the wall before putting your skates on. Turn your leg in, keep the heel on the ground, and the knee locked. Lean

Calf Stretch with Skates   *Hamstring Stretch*

forward slowly until you feel a tightness in the back of the leg. Hold this position for approximately ten to fifteen seconds and then release slowly. Repeat this at least ten times on each leg before skating.

As an alternative, this exercise can be done with skates on. Again it is important that this be done slowly.

Hamstring Stretch

The second group of muscles to stretch are the hamstrings—the four muscles in the back of the thighs. Merely touching your toes is inadequate because the action applies a great deal of stress to the lower back and does not stretch all muscles involved. To stretch these muscles properly, elevate the leg approximately two to three feet on a stool, table, or rail and turn the leg in. Bend down slowly trying to touch your toe with your knee straight. Whether you touch your toes or not is of no significance. If you feel a pulling when you are halfway down, that is adequate. Don't stop at the first sign of stretch. Continue down until you feel a healthy pull. Hold this position for approximately ten to fifteen seconds.

Next, rotate the leg so the foot is pointing upward. Resume the stretch, holding it for ten to fifteen seconds. You will feel the pull transfer from the back outside part of the leg over the midthigh. Then rotate the leg so the foot is pointing outward, and resume the stretch again for about ten to fifteen seconds.

Repeat this approximately ten to fifteen times on each leg before beginning skating. The calf and hamstring exercises are the most critical ones before you start to skate.

Quadriceps Stretch

The quadriceps, the muscles in the front of the thigh, are very critical in keeping the knee straight and allowing normal forward motion. If these muscles are weak, the knee will not be straight; it might wobble and result in knee pain.

To stretch this muscle, pull the leg behind the thigh, until you feel a stretch in the front part of the leg. Hold this position for a count of ten to fifteen seconds.

Do this approximately five to six times and repeat on the other leg.

Adductor Stretch

The adductor muscle group on the inside thigh is used extensively when skating backward. To stretch these muscles effectively, stand with your legs two to three feet apart. To stretch the right adductors, bend the left leg shifting weight over to the left foot. You will notice a very significant stretch to these inside very large muscles. Especially if you are planning a great deal of backward skating, it is essential to stretch this muscle on both thighs. Stretch for fifteen to twenty seconds and repeat at least five to ten times, depending on the specific skating events required.

Trunk Twisters

All of the above exercises are very specific and are designed for injury-free skating. It is not enough merely to bounce around with no objective in mind. Additional limbering-up exercises can also be very, very helpful before skating. This can be done with a series of trunk twisters, side-to-side bends, and so forth. Be aware, however, that the muscle groups that re-

Trunk Twisters

quire the most work must be stretched the most thoroughly. Flexibility is essential for good skating and thorough enjoyment of the sport.

STRENGTH EXERCISES

Although flexibility is a critical factor in good skating, muscle strength is also very important. Because certain muscles in the leg and low back tend to be weaker than others, the avid skater should begin a strength exercise program. These exercises take minimal time and provide excellent benefits.

The muscles in the back of the leg (the calf muscles and the hamstrings) tend to be fairly strong on their own because of walking activities in daily life. The muscles that generally require strengthening are the abdominal muscles, the quadricep muscles in the front of the thigh, and the extensor or front leg muscles.

Sit-ups

Sit-ups have been around for many years, but they are often done improperly. Doing sit-ups with your legs straight uses abdominal muscles and hip muscles, even though these hip muscles require stretching, not strengthening. Bent-leg sit-ups, however, strengthen the abdominal muscles alone. Sit-ups should be done with the heels touching the buttocks and knees flexed. Most people are unable to sit up all the way, but this is not necessary. If one finds it too difficult to sit up, move the heels back a few inches from the buttocks.

Quadriceps Strengtheners

Quadriceps strength is essential for good skating. This is especially true for the growing child and women, who have a problem with this muscle because of the angulation of the hip. The quadricep locks the knee in a straight position and holds it there. In the past, quadriceps exercises have been done with the foot dangling over the edge of a table. A weight is applied to the foot and the leg is extended. This is not a good way to strengthen this muscle, because it is possible to do damage to the knee cartilage. Whenever the quadricep muscle contracts, the knee-

Incorrect Quadriceps Stretch

cap is used as a fulcrum for lifting the leg into a fully extended position; when the leg remains in that position, there is roughly ten times the stress on the kneecap cartilage as when you are standing normally. (For the same reason, full squats have also been removed from most exercise programs.)

There is a much simpler and more effective way of strengthening the quadriceps muscle. Sit against a wall with the hip flexed and the leg straight. Add two- to five-pound weighted anklets around the ankle and lift the leg. This should be repeated at least ten to fifteen times on each leg and there should be significant resistance to the lifting. When this exercise is done properly, you can feel the stress to this particular muscle. Done properly, this quadricep muscle will strengthen and stabilize the knee during skating. The most efficient way of strengthening front leg muscles is to sit on the end of a table and place a pail

Correct Quadriceps Stretch

with sand (or skate) in it on the foot. First, lift the toes and foot up (without moving the knee), relax, and then move the foot from side to side. No damage is done to the knee since the knee is not moving. Strengthening these foot and leg muscles is most beneficial to all turning maneuvers.

PREVENTING INJURIES

Most skating injuries can be avoided by doing the strength and flexibility exercises in this chapter. However, there are certain injuries that require special preventive measures both in equipment and technique.

Warm Down

Even if you dutifully hold to the exercise regimen outlined here, your muscles will tend to contract and "tighten up" when you skate for any length of time. Thus, you should repeat the exercises *after* skating to insure against those nagging aches and pains that occur between skating sessions.

Skater's Knee

The most common problem for skaters is referred to as "skater's knee." This problem results from skating turns aggressively without proper leg strength and poor foot mechanics that cause too much leg rotation. If this problem is recurrent, try the following: Take two wedges of felt that are higher on the inside and place them in the heels of both boots. This will force your foot to the outside part of the boot and prevent it from flattening out as much and twisting. If this does not solve the problem, seek help from a sports podiatrist or orthopedist who has an interest in skating.

Blisters, Corns, and Calluses

When you develop a blister or callus, the cause will often be a loose seam in the boot, a rolled-up sock, or an ill-fitting boot. The boot should fit snugly, but not too tight. The laces should be tied tightly so as to prevent the foot from moving around in the boot, but not tightly enough to cut off circulation.

If you begin to notice irritation, moleskin, a tape-like material that can be purchased over the counter, should reduce it. However, allowing friction to continue is not a good idea. Many people develop bone spurs on their toes and on the bottom of their feet, and constant pressure on these bone spurs and the skin will result in a corn or callus. If they are very painful while skating, you should seek medical attention.

Another possible solution is a layer of "spenco" on the bottom of the boot. This is specially-designed material which will absorb pressure and friction. It can be purchased in any athletic shoe store and can often be very beneficial in reducing blister and callus formation.

Special Women's Problems

Because of the high-heeled shoes that women wear in day-to-day activities, skating in a lower boot might present problems to the back of the leg. Women should pursue an aggressive stretching program and, if necessary, a quarter-inch felt shoelift can be placed in the boot to alleviate some pressure on the back of the leg.

PART 6

SKATOLOGY

17

Be a Good Skate Buyer

Whether you are buying a pair of roller skates or renting for the first time, it is important to understand the design and function of each part of the skate. Ten years ago, you could walk into a department store and, if you were lucky, you might have had a choice of two or three styles. Now, you not only have the department stores, but specialty skate shops as well: your choices are vast and, at first glance, terribly confusing, for the novice as well as for the more advanced skater. The seventies have become the age of component buying—this concept has even spread to the roller-skating industry. However, with few exceptions, all roller skating components are universally interchangeable.

A roller skate is composed of seven basic parts—wheels, bearings, trucks, plates, pivots, boots, and toe stops. Let's look at each of these parts individually and then at how they fit together as a whole.

The Wheel

Roller-skating wheels come in a variety of heights, widths, and compositions, as well as a vast array of colors. There are new hard plastic compounds for indoor wheels and new polyurethane compositions for outdoor wheels. The polyurethane compositions of today's outdoor wheels have brought about the biggest change in skating over the past decade. The metal wheels of yesteryear offered a rough and sometimes dangerous

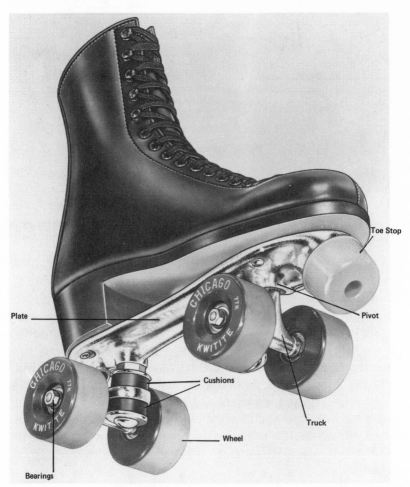

The modern roller skate (Chicago Roller Skate Company)

ride over concrete streets and sidewalks. The switch to the softer, synthetic polyurethane wheel by skateboarders in the late sixties has been adopted by the roller-skating industry, offering a smoother and quieter ride for all—as well as greater traction and more maneuverability. There is now a wheel that is best suited for every skater's needs—skating surface, style, skill, and financial considerations are all factors to consider.

Ball Bearings

The ball bearings are very small steel balls, which enable the wheels to spin. There are two types—*loose* and *precision*. Loose bearings go on a threaded axle. Race nuts are first threaded on the axle, then the bearings, then another race nut—there is a lot of metal involved. Loose bearings are less expensive than precision bearings, but they are also more susceptible to embedded dirt and therefore require frequent cleaning. Another problem is that as the wheel spins, heat is generated, causing loose bearings to expand and abrade. If not readjusted often, eventually they will strip the axle, and the whole part will have to be replaced.

Precision bearings are sealed off, so that it is quite difficult for dirt to infiltrate. They are also packed in grease, so that they don't require lubrication as often as loose bearings do, and they are quieter. Precision bearings are a bit more expensive than loose bearings, but they don't require constant attention and maintenance, and they last longer.

Trucks

The truck connects the wheels on their axle to the plate on the bottom of the roller skate. The truck absorbs shock and provides the steering mechanism. When viewed from the front of the skate, the truck appears triangular in shape; from the side it appears V-shaped. The top of the truck is joined to the boot plate by a pivot—this is the steering mechanism. On the bottom of the truck (the bottom of the V), a *king pin* passes through a flat, circular hole—this is the shock absorber section of the truck. Cushions are inserted on the king pin—either one or two—and rest on either one or both sides of the truck. A two-cushion (or *double-action*) truck absorbs shock and vibration better than a one-cushion or single-action truck, as well as providing greater maneuverability. They are also more expensive, but is that any surprise?

Pivots

The top of the truck connects to the plate at the pivot. There are two types of pivots—ball-and-socket pivots and pivot insertions. Ball-and-socket pivots are very expensive and are found only on a forged-type plate. Forged plates also occasionally have adjustable pivots, making their movement independent of truck adjustment. Ball-and-socket pivots are a better choice for the figure skater, as they allow greater precision in movement. For the average skater, though, pivot insertions are more than adequate. They are generally used on all medium- and lower-priced trucks. Pivots are not purchased separately—your choice of pivot will depend on your choice of plate and vice versa.

Plates

The plate is the slab of metal—usually aluminum or an aluminum alloy—which connects the boot to the rest of the skate. There are three types of plates:

Forged plates are heavier and stronger than the others. The extra weight is an advantage for figure skaters because they can get extra momentum once moving and therefore smoothness—it is a disadvantage in long-distance or speed skating where the extra weight slows down the skater and wears him out more quickly. The forged plate is also distinguished by a jump bar connecting the hangers (the protruding part of the bottom of the plate to which the trucks connect). This adds strength to the plate, a vital feature for more "radical" skaters (that is, skate parks, jumping). Other features of the forged plate include an adjustable toe stop and, occasionally, adjustable pivots. Basically, the forged plate is a deluxe model plate for more experienced skaters or more radical ones. They are quite expensive and are not necessary for the average or intermediate skater.

Unlike the forged plate, *sand-cast* and *die-cast* plates are a one-piece design. The jump bar of the forged plate is replaced by a ridge that is cast into the plate itself, connecting the two hangers. Of the two, the sand-cast plate is stronger and is used on most medium-priced skates. The sand-cast plate is lighter weight than a forged plate, but weight varies from brand to brand.

Die-cast plates are not as strong as either the forged or the sand-cast, but are the least expensive of the three types and are also light-weight—great for speed skating and long-distance skating. Unlike the forged and sand-cast plates, which are usually polished on both sides, die-cast plates are often polished on only one, leaving some rough edges. The skater must be careful of the rough edges or he could get cut.

On both the sand-cast and die-cast plates, toe stops are non-adjustable and pivot bushings are used. For radical skating, jump bars can be added to either type for added strength and safety when making jumps and hard landings.

Boots

A good boot will offer both support and comfort. There are many boots on the market to choose from—everything from the traditional pro-style, high-quality leather boot to the new "jogger" type skate boot to inexpensive vinyl boots. There are also an increasing number of places that offer custom-made boots. Roller-skating shops, like Skates on Haight in San Francisco, will mount the wheels, trucks and plates of your choice on anything from hiking boots to sneakers to your old, but comfortable, pair of hush puppies.

Your hush puppies offer comfort, but not good ankle support. The best boot to buy, particularly for the beginning skater, is a boot that comes right above the ankle. Depending on your pocketbook, this includes everything from the least expensive, unlined vinyl boot to the best top-grain leather boot. The higher quality leather boots offer greater comfort and longer life. The new, lightweight, running-shoe type skating boot—particularly popular with outdoor skaters because of the obvious tie-in with the running craze—offer no ankle support and are best for more experienced skaters or for those skaters with strong ankles built up in other sports. Good ankle support is not only vital for the beginner; it is also very important for figure and dance skaters who need this support to execute jumps and spins.

The beginning skater need not immediately go out and buy the finest quality and most expensive leather boot on the market. There are now quite a few low-to-medium priced skate boots available that offer comfort, support, and durability without inflicting too big a dent on the skater's pocketbook. A worthy suggestion from Skates on Haight is, when on limited funds, invest in higher quality wheels and bearings and a less expensive boot.

Toe Stops

No skater should be without a set of toe stops. The toe stops have three functions:

1. They can be used to stop when skating backward or very slowly forward.

2. They are an essential pivot in artistic, disco, and trick skating.

3. They offer protection to the toe of the boot.

Toe stops come in all shapes, sizes, colors, and flexibilities. The best toe stop for a beginning skater is a bull's-eye—a large cylindrical toe stop. The larger the toe stop the more protection it offers the boot and the easier it is to use it to stop (though it does cut down on maneuverability). The harder the toe stop the more durable it is—this is particularly good for outdoor skating where skating surfaces are more abrasive.

The shape of a toe stop is a matter of individual preference, as well as skating style. According to Joe Nazzaro, perhaps the premier skating expert in the country today and owner of Western Skate Sales in Menlo Park, California, the spring of a toe stop is of particular importance in indoor skating. Teachers will often suggest a particular toe stop to a student to complement or offset his or her particular style of jumping or spinning.

Good leather roller skate boots (Riedel Boot Company).

Now let's take some questions from the floor:

How do I choose a wheel?

Choosing a wheel is not difficult if you know exactly what type of skating you will be doing and where you're going to be doing it. For indoor skating, a plastic compound or hard polyurethane wheel is best. Designed for a smooth, flat surface, they are also longer-lasting and generally less expensive than your softer outdoor wheels. The hard polyurethane wheels are also more versatile than the soft wheel—they can be used outdoors, although on rough pavement they give a rougher and more slippery ride.

For outdoor skating, a softer polyurethane wheel is a better choice. The softer wheel is more resilient (has more bounce) but can still stand up to more "radical" skating surfaces. The softness absorbs any irregularities in the skating surface—and the shock. Soft wheels offer a smoother, quieter ride, better traction, and greater speed on uneven surfaces. In bicycling, when you race on rough roads you deflate your tires down to about ninety pounds of pressure. When racing on a smooth surface, they should be inflated up to about 120 pounds of pressure. So it is also in roller skating.

Don't the softer wheels wear down rapidly?

Yes, they do tend to wear down faster and are more expensive as well, but durability and cost vary from manufacturer to manufacturer. Durability will also vary with the skating surface. If you use your soft wheel on a fairly smooth surface, they will last a great deal longer than if you are continually skating on rough asphalt. The most important consideration when buying your wheels is this: Are they a proper composition for the terrain that you'll be skating? Only if the answer is yes can you expect the wheels to deliver the maximum in performance.

Keep one other very important thing in mind. In roller skating, as in any industry, there is quality and there is garbage—and then there is a whole lot in between. Just because a wheel is soft does not mean that there is not a better and more durable soft wheel for outdoor skating. And just because a wheel is hard, it does not mean that there isn't a better hard wheel on the market for indoor skating. There are considerations other than a wheel's softness or hardness to your touch that must be considered when judging quality.

How can I judge the quality of a wheel?

Don't go by price alone. A good test of quality in an outdoor wheel is the bounce test. When comparing wheels, bounce them. Two wheels that may have felt awfully close in composition to your touch may act completely differently when bounced. The wheel with more bounce is more resilient; it will last longer and give you better performance.

Another good test of quality in a wheel is craftsmanship. Look at the back edge of the wheel—are there bubbles or is it clear and smooth? How is the outside machining? Is the wheel consistent? Is the inside of the wheel where the bearings will be seated round, or are there small chunks of urethane torn here and there? Your eye can tell you a lot about quality—trust it!

What about height and width when choosing a wheel? Is this an important consideration?

Height is always associated with speed and width with traction. Wheels vary in width from 60 mm to 70 mm. The wider wheels grip a rough road surface better and give greater speed with less effort, but restrict precision movement that is so vital in dance and artistic skating. On the other hand, a narrower wheel, while giving the skater more maneuverability, requires a greater expenditure of energy for speed and distance skating on regular surfaces. For any type of skating where speed is important, a higher than average wheel is best.

For Sunday afternoons in the park or on the boardwalk, a wide wheel of average height is the best choice. For the skater who wants to do trick skating or dance skating, the narrow wheel is more suitable. Evaluate your needs and purchase a wheel that best suits them.

Do precision bearings ever need to be replaced?

Precision bearings require a lot less maintenance than do loose bearings. (For specific maintenance guidelines see the next chapter on skate maintenance.) Even precision bearings wear out eventually, though—just not as fast as the loose bearings. Boardwalk skaters in Venice use precision bearings for the most part and the sand and dirt still get inside and eventually wear them out.

How tightly or loosely should I adjust my trucks?

Trucks should be adjusted according to a skater's skill, the maneuverability desired for a particular type of skating, and the terrain. A tighter truck is appropriate for the novice skater who has not yet gained a great deal of confidence or control over his motions on wheels. On a beginning skater, a skate with loose trucks seems to have a mind of its own. Like putting a new driver in a finely tuned Cadillac with power steering—one small movement has a big effect.

Until you gain more control over your skates keep the trucks fairly tight—this will give you the greatest control, if not the most maneuverability. A tighter truck also gives more support for the long distance skater or speed skater, and more stability for the jump skater or ramp rider. Kenny Means, champion "radical" skate park skater, keeps his trucks so tight that the cushions bulge out of the caps. In speed or long distance skating, forward motion matters most—you don't want to worry about your skates going in other directions.

Looser trucks are desirable for more experienced skaters, who can manipulate and control their skates. Looser trucks also offer the skater more maneuverability in any kind of dance skating, or wherever more complicated spins are to be performed.

What are the advantages of an adjustable toe stop?

An adjustable toe stop allows for different height settings for different types of skating and different levels of ability. A beginning skater is better off with the toe stop adjusted fairly low—though not so low that it may inadvertently drag on the ground (for example, when pointing the toe on the free leg). Also, with adjustable toe stops, as the toe stops wear out, you can adjust them downwards accordingly. As with other equipment in skating, choose and adjust your toe stops according to your ability and style.

What do I look for when buying a boot?

There are five basic parts to a roller skating boot—the sole, the counter, the uppers, the tongue, and the outside of the boot

The many types of roller skates now on the market (Sure-Grip International).

itself. The *sole* is the foundation of the boot. It should be firm and quite inflexible. The *counter* is attached to the sole of the boot—its main purpose is to provide support for the heel and the sides of the feet, as well as arch support. It consists of a heel cup as well as a firm leather instep, which stops at the ball of the foot. The *uppers* work with the counter to keep the foot firmly in place, to provide ankle support and for protection. In order for the uppers to do their job, the laces must be strong and tightly laced. The boot should feel snug—still allowing adequate ankle movement. Whichever boot you decide on should have a well-padded *tongue*—this protects the foot from lace-burn when the boot is laced up tightly. The *outside of the boot* can vary from inexpensive vinyl to high-grade leather. Whatever the material, the hooks and eyelets on the boot should be well-secured so that they don't pop loose when the laces are pulled tight.

Another measure of quality to look for, when buying a boot, plate, truck combination, is whether the boot is bolted, as opposed to riveted, to the plate. Riveting has become the most popular method of attachment, as rivets take less time to put in —making it easier to meet mass demand and competitive pricing. If your skates are going to get a lot of use and some hard wear, request a shoe with a bolted plate—riveted plates may come off in "radical" skating situations.

How should the boot feel?

Take your time when trying on a pair of roller skates. Your toes should come up as far as possible to the front of the boot without discomfort. From a quarter to three-eighths of an inch is about the maximum amount of room that should be allowed. If the boot feels somewhat snug across the ball of the foot or at the back of the ankle, don't worry—after several spins around the park or rink, the leather will loosen up. If the skate feels much too narrow, try either a wider width or a half-size larger. Most importantly, don't judge the fit of a boot until it's completely laced up—only then can you be a good judge of the boot's comfort and support.

The height of ankle boots does vary slightly. As a general rule, the boot should not cover any of the muscles in the back of the leg—about an inch above the ankle is a good height.

What about buying skates for children?

For a very young child just starting out, buy a pair of very inexpensive plastic skates that are strapped on. This will give the child a chance to try out some "wheels," to see if they like it. If the "wheels" go over really big and you decide to invest some money in a good pair of skates for your child, you have a couple of alternatives. You can buy a plate, truck, and wheel assembly that is a bit too large for your child's boot and as his foot grows just buy new boots. Or you can buy entire new skate assemblies as his foot grows, always buying them a half-size too large and replacing them only as he's growing out of them. A skate that is a half-size too big will still allow a fit that is snug enough to give proper support and comfort.

18

Tuning Up Your Skates - Maintenance

Zipping through the park on a warm Sunday afternoon, suddenly you feel a wobble in your skate that you know shouldn't be there. Or there's a groan coming from a wheel that wasn't groaning last week. Or suddenly your usually brainless left skate seems to have found a mind of its own. What do you do?

There is not much you can do to keep sliding along if you've let the maintenance on your skates slide for too long. To get the most enjoyment out of your skates, it's of the utmost importance to understand how to take care of them. Check out your skates each and every time you use them. Tune them up every six months. If maintenance becomes a part of your skating routine, your skates will give you many years of good wear. Let's take a look at the do's and don't's of skate maintenance.

Keep Your Wheels Rolling

Spin the wheels on your skates—make sure they spin smoothly and quietly. If they wobble, if they seem to hesitate at points, or if there is a cracking or grinding sound, your wheels aren't in tip-top shape. If the problem is uneven rotation, either you need to tighten your wheels or you have a bent axle. Tightening the wheels is no problem—this should be done every time you skate anyway. If a bent axle is your problem, you'll have to invest in a new part; this can be obtained from your local rink or skate shop. Hard falls can bend axles; if you do a lot of hard falling, you should buy sturdier truck assemblies.

Excessive noise from your wheels is an indication that they probably need to be cleaned and oiled. Loose bearings, particularly if used outdoors, should be cleaned at least once every month, for they offer the wheel little or no protection against dirt, sand, grime, and everything else that's not supposed to be there. To clean them, take the bearings off the skate, use a damp towel or a cleaning solvent to get all of the impurities out, and then put them back on. Loose bearings also like a drop of lightweight oil now and then—about every ten to fifteen times you use them will do—but never oil without cleaning first.

Precision bearings are a double-sealed bearing and don't pose all the problems that loose bearings do—they are insulated from 'the outside, making it very difficult for the impurities to infiltrate. Every six months to a year, depending on how often you skate, have your rink or skate shop clean and repack the bearings in grease. Make this a part of your periodic skate "tune-up."

Generally, indoor skaters do not have to clean their wheels and bearings as often as outdoor skaters, but it should not be neglected. Bearings get dirty even on a well-kept, smooth skating surface.

Speed skating boot (Chicago Roller Skate Co.).

Truck Adjustment

After checking the wheels on your skates, check your trucks. Tight trucks will give the skater the greatest amount of control, while loose trucks give the skater the greatest amount of maneuverability. Trucks should be adjusted differently according to ability, skating style, and terrain. The beginning skater should adjust the trucks more tightly, for better ankle support and more control. More advanced skaters, either indoor or outdoor, particularly dance and figure skaters, can safely adjust their trucks more loosely, without fear of spraining an ankle. How can you tell whether your trucks are too light or too loose?

Trucks are too tight if they don't respond properly to shifts of weight or body lean. On the other hand, if your skates seem to have a life of their own, or if they wobble, your trucks are too loose. Adjust them one-half turn with a wrench—try them out. Continue doing this until they feel right. If your trucks are too tight, do the opposite of the above. When loosening a truck, it is important to first loosen the locknut away from the hanger with a wrench, then tighten the king pin with a screwdriver—this is to insure that the king pin doesn't come loose as the truck is loosened, causing the trucks to come off. Adjust, try out, readjust util the skates feel comfortable.

All trucks on your skates should be set equally tight or loose. If your trucks, or one of your trucks, consistently lean to the side, in spite of your truck adjustment, check for a bent king pin—if this is the case, replace it.

Trucks will loosen up much faster in outdoor skating than in indoor skating. The outdoor skater may want to carry a small wrench in his pocket if he's planning a full day's skating. A set of tools for skate adjustment may be purchased from your rink or skate shop.

Cushions (Making Sure Your "Shocks" Are Absorbing)

Check the cushions in your skates. Cushions are extremely important; they allow for action or movement in the skate, as well as acting as shock absorbers. When the cushions are compressed, they bulge out. After a lot of wear, the cushions may crack, which will affect the steering. At that time, they should be replaced. Never replace just one or two cushions—replace them all. To replace them, loosen the king pin until it comes off the plate, remove the truck and the locknut from the plate, and then slide the cushions off of the assembly. Replace the cushions and reassemble.

Adjustable Ball Pivots

The adjustable ball pivot thread, found in your more expensive, forged plates, has a tendency to wear down. This wears the hanger out and throws the action off completely. To check the ball pivots, take the truck and bring it straight up and down. If you hear it click, you know that it needs to be adjusted with a pivot wrench. Pivots should always be adjusted after adjusting the trucks.

Toe Stops

Toe stops should be adjusted so that they are easy and comfortable to use without dragging on the ground. On an adjustable toe stop, there is a small bolt on the side that locks it into position. Experiment some, see what feels the best.

Whatever height you decide on, your toe stops should be twisted around as they wear down. Nonadjustable toe stops can also be loosened and twisted around by loosening the bolt at the end of the toe stop. (When they become very worn down, they should be replaced.) After adjusting make sure that the toe stops are securely fastened into place.

Boot Care

The worst problem in boot care is foot perspiration, which causes an adverse chemical reaction with the leather. No matter how good the leather, it will eventually dry out. A good foot powder can help to alleviate this problem.

Your boots will last much longer if you leave them open and dry them out naturally after each use. Don't leave them in the trunk of your car until the next time you skate—they won't dry properly. Another common mistake is to leave socks in the boot while they dry. When you are finished skating, loosen the laces, and let your boots dry in the air. Don't dry them near heat—this is also bad for the leather. Use a good leather polish and preserver on your boots occasionally.

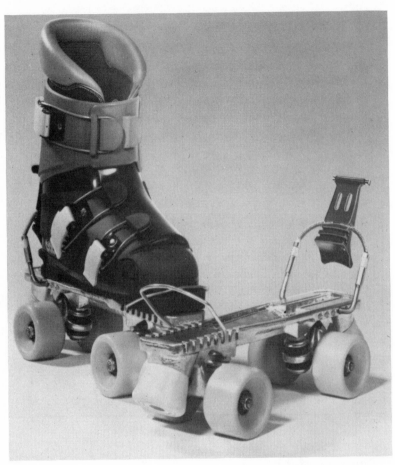

Skiers can practice their sport year-round with these skates (Sure-Grip International).

Finally, check regularly to see that the boot is securely fastened to the boot plate. This is particularly important if the boot is riveted rather than bolted to the plate.

Clean Your Skates

After checking your skates thoroughly, make sure that every part of your skate is clean. When they are clean they will not only perform better, but you will find it easier to spot problems. Not only bearings need cleaning—the trucks, plates, boots, toe stops, and all other parts of the skate should be kept clean. And you don't need fancy cleaning solutions—just a damp towel.

More Maintenance Hints

• *During the "breaking-in" period—the first twenty to thirty hours of skating time—unlace and lace your boots all the way each time you go skating. As your boot breaks in, the leather expands—the lacing must change each time in order to maintain the proper tension and proper fit.*

• *Don't ride through water or in the rain. It may seem romantic to roll in the rain with the one you love, but it's dangerous for you and bad for your skates. Water causes urethane wheels to lose traction, making for a very slippery ride, and may destroy the bearings, which makes for a slippery pocketbook. Not only does water cause the bearings to rust, but it will act as a leaching agent, sucking all the necessary grease and leaving you with very rough sounding bearings, a very noisy skate and an uneven roll. Water also deteriorates the rubber cushions and ruins the leather. So stay away from water! (Sand and dirt aren't so hot for your skates either.)*

• *As a final note, rotate your wheels periodically—just like you do on your car. The front, inside wheel wears down the fastest; if you rotate the wheels occasionally, you will compensate for the excessive wear on this part.*

A Quick Check List

Every time you skate you should check that:

1. the boot is securely fastened to the boot plate
2. the wheels spin quietly and evenly
3. the trucks are adjusted properly for your skating ability and terrain
4. the king pin is securely screwed into the bottom of the plate.

A monthly check should include:

1. checking toe stops for wear—rotate them down (if you have adjustable toe stops) or around (if they are nonadjustable)

No, it's not done with mirrors.

2. cleaning your skate thoroughly—while cleaning you will spot areas that need maintenance

3. checking for any bends or cracks in your king pins, trucks, axles, or cushions.

Your six month or yearly "tune-up" should include:

1. rotating the wheels

2. repacking precision bearings in grease

3. assessing your skating needs—is your skating style still compatible with your equipment? If the parts of your skate show signs of excessive wear, maybe you should invest in more rugged equipment.

If you are the lazy type and don't feel like giving your skates the thorough cleaning and tune-ups that they periodically need, let your rink or local roller skating shop do it for you. They will check out every part of your skate, give each part a thorough cleaning, and will rotate the wheels for you at the same time. The cost of having someone else do it will pay for itself in the long run—in the added enjoyment that you will get out of your skates as well as the money you save from parts that don't have to be replaced as often.

19

How to Rent Your Rollers

What should you expect from the skates you rent from the roller rink or from your local skate shop? There are advantages and disadvantages to renting rather than buying skates. An obvious advantage in renting skates, particularly for the beginner, is that you will have to make no large lump investment in a pair of skates. Not only is renting skates inexpensive, but you can enjoy it without having to worry about deciding among the vast—and getting vaster—amount of equipment on the market.

The obvious drawback to renting a pair of skates is that the skates have been broken in by as many different pairs of feet as have rented them—everyone with a different shaped foot. Like running in someone else's running shoes or playing golf with someone else's clubs, you will not feel as comfortable with rental equipment or enjoy it as much as you would equipment that's been custom-fitted and custom-adjusted to your own needs.

The adjustment of the trucks will also vary every time you rent skates. As noted in the previous chapter, truck adjustment should vary with ability, skating style, and terrain. You will enjoy skating more if your skates are adjusted according to your skating needs. When you rent, you may get a tightly adjusted truck one week and a loosely adjusted truck the next. One way to deal with this problem is to carry a small wrench with you so that you can adjust the trucks every time you rent a pair of skates—it may take some time to get them adjusted the way that you want them, though.

When renting, you can ask the rink operator or shop manager to give you a more tightly or loosely adjusted truck. If you're renting, chances are you're a beginner, and your best bet in terms of comfort and safety is to stick with a fairly tightly adjusted truck. Most rinks and rental shops adjust for the beginner.

Rental skates, for the most part, are of good quality. They are built and sold for the specific purpose of rental wear, which means long-term wear. Therefore, rental wheels will be a harder polyurethane than many polyurethanes on the market. (If you decide to buy a pair of skates for outdoor skating, you may want to invest in a softer wheel which will give you a smoother ride but less wear.)

Shop for a good place to rent your roller skates. Compare skates and prices at several rental places—some will have better wheels and will take better care of their skates than others. Specialty skate shops generally buy high-quality rental skates, and claim they check the rental skates out daily—to make sure that they are clean and in good working order. Rinks and rental shops will generally feel a greater responsibility to their customers than a more tenuous operation like a skate rental truck.

Cheapskates (Venice, California)

A farewell tune . . . .

A Mexican Hat Dance on Wheels

Some shops, like Skates on Haight in San Francisco, offer skating safety clinics for their customers.

Safety equipment, such as knee pads, gloves, helmets, and elbow pads, should be available for rental wherever you rent your skates. More esoteric equipment (padded shorts, skating outfits) is generally sold, not rented. If you are a very nervous beginning skater, you would be wise to rent at least some gloves and knee pads when you rent your skates.

The "Wall of Wheels" at Skates on Haight

Renter's Hints

1. Spin the wheels—make sure that they spin smoothly and that they are clean and well oiled.

2. Look for a wheel that is fairly wide and feels resilient. If a wheel is too hard it won't cushion the joints and it won't grip the road—it's too slick.

3. Make sure the wheels aren't chipped and that they are perfectly round. There should be no flat spots and they should feel smooth to the touch.

4. For the beginner, trucks should be rather tightly adjusted—for better ankle support and more control.

5. The toe stop should be healthy—it shouldn't be so worn down that you can't use it.

6. Make sure the laces on the boots aren't so worn that they are about to break in spots—you should be able to pull the laces real tight without them breaking. Also, make sure the laces will give you plenty of room to tie them once they are laced all the way up; if not, they will keep coming undone while you are skating, or you will end up tying them before you've laced the boots all of the way up. This will not give you the ankle support that you need.

Glossary

Action—The amount of maneuverability or play adjusted into the truck of the roller skate.

Axel—A one-and-one-half revolution jump, taking off from a forward edge and landing on a backward edge.

Bracket turn—A one-foot turn from a forward edge to the opposite backward edge (or vice versa), in which the rotation of the body is against the original edge.

Chasse—A stroke accomplished by raising one skate from the floor alongside the other.

Choctaw turn—A 180-degree half-turn from a forward edge to the opposite backward edge.

Counter—A one-foot turn from a forward edge to a similar backward edge (or vice versa); rotation of the body is counter to the direction of the original edge.

Crossover—A skating maneuver in which one leg is crossed in front of or behind the other.

Cusp—(1) The midpoint of a three turn. (2) In figure skating circle eights, the point where the long axis intersects the circumference of the circle.

Edge—The curved line of direction to left or right that results from body lean and weight transfer on the skate.

Flat—(1) A straight line of direction resulting from body weight placed directly over the center of the skate. (2) A deformed wheel.

Free leg—The leg not in contact with the skating surface.

Long axis—The imaginary line running lengthwise through a circle eight or serpentine, dissecting the circles into equal parts.

Loop—(1) The smaller elliptical figure in the figure circles. (2) A kind of jump in freestyle skating.

Loose bearings—A type of wheel bearing assembly in which the bearings are not sealed off.

Mapes jump—A toe-assisted jump that takes off backwards, in which body rotation is with the take-off edge.

Mohawk turn—A two-foot, 180-degree half-turn from a forward edge to a similar backward edge.

Plate—On a skate, the slab of metal that connects the boot to the rest of the skate.

Pivot—The part of a roller skate where the truck and plate are connected.

Precision bearings—Bearings that are sealed off and packed in grease inside the wheel.

Rocker—A one-foot turn from a forward edge to a similar backward edge (or vice versa); rotation is in same direction as the original edge.

Rotary push—The body windup used in starts of backward-edge circles.

Salchow—A full-turn jump from a forward to opposite backward edge.

Serpentine—A three-circle figure.

Short axis—The imaginary line that crosses the long axis at the point of tangency of two circles.

Side-push—The basic forward skating stroke.

Spin—Three continuous rotations around a stationary axis.

Slalom—Skating curves in and out between a line of pylons.

Split position—The in-the-air spread of both legs extended.

Stag position—The in-the-air position of one leg extended straight out behind and the other leg tucked under.

"T" position—The starting position in forward skating—the heel of one skate is placed near the instep of the other, forming a "T."

"T" stop—The basic forward-skating stop in which the free skate is brought behind the skating leg on the skating surface.

Three turn—A one-foot turn named for the shape of the resulting curve.

Truck—The part of the roller skate that connects the axle and wheels to the plate and that absorbs shock and provides the steering mechanism of the skate.

For Further Exploration

Associations

Roller Skating Rink Operators Association (RSROA), 7700 "A" Street, Lincoln, Nebraska 68510. The RSROA will provide you with information on every aspect of roller skating: events, people, rink locations, instructional material, proficiency tests, etc. The United States Amateur Confederation (USAC), a division of the RSROA, publishes a series of pamphlets on roller skating competitions, rules, and classifications of movements in dance, freestyle, figures, speed, roller hockey, etc.

Publications

Skate magazine. Published quarterly by the RSROA at the above address, the magazine covers events, competitions, skaters, and equipment, nationally and internationally.

Roller Skating magazine, Box 1028, Dana Point, California 92629. A lively bimonthly, covering the California skating "scene," disco, interviews, personalities, etc.

Manufacturers

Chicago Skate Co.
4458 W. Lake Street
Chicago, Illinois 60624

M & K Industries
171 Marion Street
Buffalo, New York 14207

Roller Derby Skate Corp.
311 Edwards Street
Litchfield, Illinois 62056

Snyder Skate Co.
2552 Titus Ave.
Dayton, Ohio 45414

Sure-Grip Skate Co.
11223 Peach Street
Lynwood, California 90262

Distributors, Consultants

Western Skate Sales
189 Constitution Drive
P.O. Box 2766
Menlo Park, California 94025

Skating Apparel

Star Styles of Miami
475 NW 42nd Avenue
Miami, Florida 33126

Boot Manufacturers

Riedell Shoes, Inc.
Industrial Park
P.O. Box 21
Red Wing, Minnesota 55066

Index

About The Authors

Hal Straus has written about sports, politics, and other twentieth-century subjects for several newspapers and periodicals. He is the Compiling Editor of the *Gymnastics Guide*. A transplanted New Yorker, he is currently working on a novel in Calabasas, California.

Marilou Sturges is a freelance photographer and writer. Her work has appeared in the *Gymnastics Guide* and other publications. She lives in Santa Monica, California.

6616

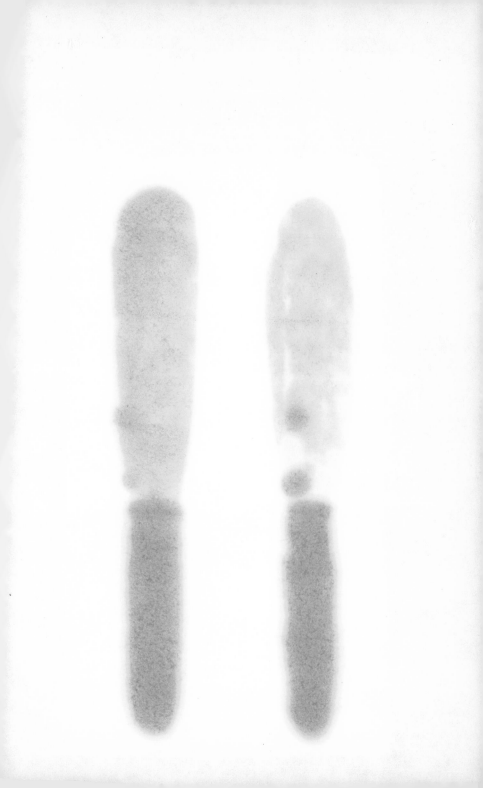

DATE DUE